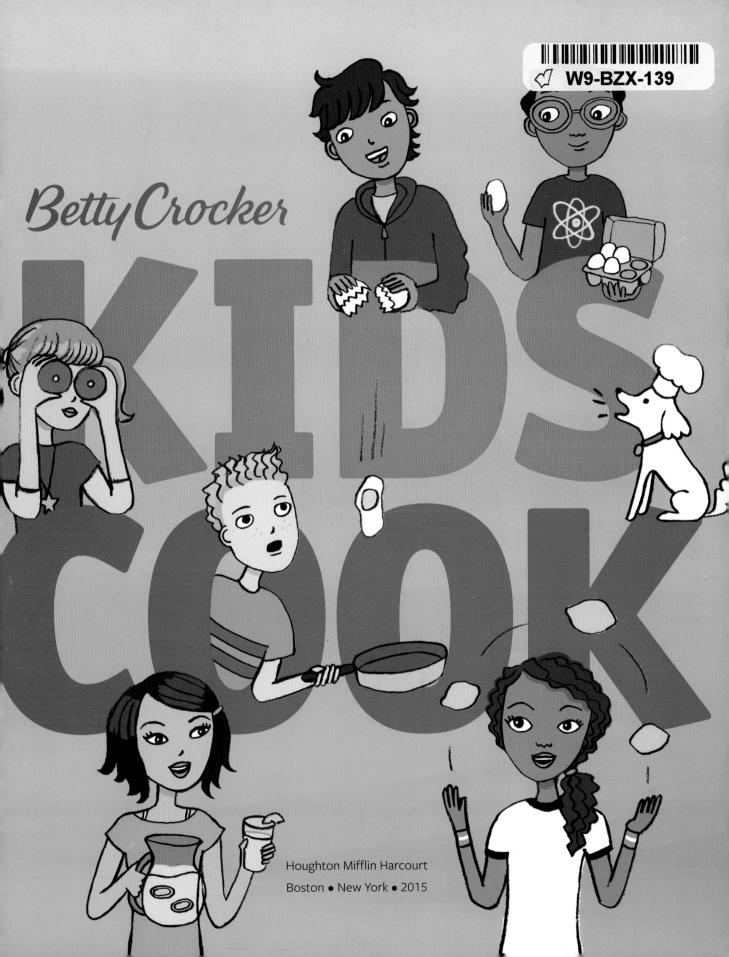

Betty Crocker

KIDS COOK

Houghton Mifflin Harcourt

Boston • New York • 2015

W9-BZX-139

GENERAL MILLS

Creative Content and Publishing Director: Elizabeth Nientimp

Food Content Marketing Manager: Heather Reid Liebo

Senior Editor: Grace Wells

Food Editor: Mary Kaye Sahli

Kitchen Manager: Ann Stuart

Recipe Development and Testing: Betty Crocker Kitchens

Photography: General Mills Photography Studios and Image Library

HOUGHTON MIFFLIN HARCOURT

Publisher: Natalie Chapman

Editorial Director: Cindy Kitchel

Executive Editor: Anne Ficklen

Editorial Associate: Molly Aronica

Managing Editor: Marina Padakis

Associate Production Editor: Helen Seachrist

Cover Design: Tai Blanche

Interior Design and Layout: Tai Blanche

Senior Production Coordinator: Kimberly Kiefer

Illustrations: Liz Adams

www.hmhco.com

Library of Congress Cataloging-in-Publication Data:

Crocker, Betty.
  Betty Crocker kids cook!
      pages cm
  Rev. ed.
  Includes index.
  ISBN 978-0-544-57002-3 (spiral bound) — ISBN 978-0-544-57003-0 (ebook)
  1. Cooking—Juvenile literature. I. Title. II. Title: Kids cook.
  TX652.5.C688 2015
  641.5—dc23

                                    2015007136

Manufactured in China

SCP 10 9 8 7 6 5 4 3 2 1

The Betty Crocker Kitchens seal guarantees success in your kitchen. Every recipe has been tested in America's Most Trusted Kitchens™ to meet our high standards of reliability, easy preparation and great taste.

FIND MORE GREAT IDEAS AT
BettyCrocker.com

Hi Families!

In the Betty Crocker Kitchens, cooking is our favorite thing—it's fun and creative, plus you end up with something good to eat too! We would love for you to join us and discover all of the joy that can come from making food in your own kitchen. This book is designed to help you do just that. *Kids Cook* is meant to help kids learn to cook, but it's for all other family members too! Whether others want to help in the kitchen or just enjoy the tasty dishes that are made, everyone plays a part in the food fun.

Although watching cooking shows and chefs on TV can be entertaining, it's much more adventurous to explore food preparation in your own kitchen. With this book filled with wonderful illustrations and photos, you'll be guided through all of the steps for making a wide variety of foods. Yes, this book is filled with yummy, fun recipes that are all easy to make. Many can be completed by kids, but we always recommend that an adult be nearby for questions and help if needed.

Look for the 🧤 that shows you something will be hot and an adult should help. Also, if there is a task that requires help such as cutting with a knife or other sharp tool, the 🔪 will show up. So be sure to watch for these signs that are there to keep you safe in the kitchen.

Be sure to check out some eating guidelines too—MyPlate on page 8 will show how to organize your plate so that eating the right things is easy. Plus, look for tips and cooking information up front before you start cooking!

So let's get started—a cooking adventure is at your fingertips!

Betty Crocker

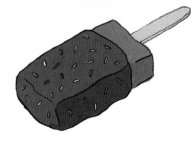

CONTENTS

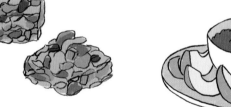

Just the Basics
Cooking Words

Here are some cooking words that you will often see in recipes. It's helpful to have this information as you start cooking in the kitchen, and the list can be referred to anytime you need to know the meaning of a word that you don't understand. You can always ask an adult about word definitions too.

Bake: Cook food in the oven using dry heat. Bake food uncovered for a dry, crisp top or covered to keep food moist. Baking is usually done at a slightly lower temperature than roasting.

Beat: Mix ingredients using a whisk, egg beater or electric mixer.

Boil: Cook liquid on top of the stove (or in the microwave) until bubbles appear on the surface.

Brown: Cook food until it looks brown on the outside.

Chop: Cut food into small pieces on a cutting board using a knife.

Cool: Let food stand at room temperature until it is the desired temperature.

Cover: Use plastic wrap, foil, waxed paper or a dish cover to enclose food in a container for storage or cooking.

Drain: Pour off liquid by putting the food in a colander or strainer. For some foods, like ground beef, you might use a spoon to scoop the liquid drippings away.

Freeze: Put food in the freezer until it is firm.

Grate: Rub a food against the smallest holes of a grater to make tiny pieces.

Grease: Coat insides of pan or dish with butter or shortening using a paper towel or pastry brush to help keep food from sticking. Cooking spray can be used also.

Knead: Work dough on floured surface with hands to make it smooth and springy.

Melt: Change a solid ingredient like chocolate or butter into a liquid by heating on the stovetop or in the microwave.

Mix: Stir ingredients with a spoon, fork, whisk or electric mixer until combined. Sometimes a blender or food processor is used to mix or puree ingredients.

Peel: Remove the outer skin of some fruits and vegetables with a knife, vegetable peeler or fingers.

Refrigerate: Put food in the refrigerator to chill it or keep it cold.

Roast: Cook meat, poultry or vegetables in the oven uncovered, often on a rack in a pan. The oven temperature is often a little higher than it is for baking.

Shred: Rub a food against the largest holes of a grater to make short, narrow strips.

Slice: Cut into flat pieces all about the same thickness using a knife.

Kitchen Talk

Yes, you should have fun in the kitchen when you cook, but there are just a few tips to help keep you safe and healthy when you are making food.

Keep It Clean

- Wash your hands with warm soapy water before starting to cook and often when you are in the kitchen.
- Wear an apron if you like to keep your clothing clean.
- Use paper towels to wipe up spills.
- Check dishes and pans before using to be sure they are clean.
- Use a different cutting board for each type of food that you cut.

Safety First

- If food needs to be cut with a knife, ask an adult to help.
- For appliances like the blender, a beater, a food processor or the microwave, ask an adult for help.
- Always have pot holders or oven mitts on hand for hot items.
- Turn handles of pans toward the center of the stove.
- Use a wooden spoon or a spoon with a handle that is not metal to stir on the stove—metal gets hot.

Measure Well

You'll want to follow the recipe you are using and be accurate with measuring. Measuring cups and spoons will be labeled as to what size they are, so check before filling. Here is a little primer on measure sizes.

1 tablespoon = 3 teaspoons
¼ cup = 4 tablespoons
½ cup = 8 tablespoons
1 cup = 16 tablespoons

- Liquid measuring cups are often glass and have marks for the amount of liquid. They come in sizes from 1 cup to 8 cups.
- Dry measuring cups each have a separate measuring amount. They come in sizes from ⅛ cup to 1 cup.

MyPlate

MyPlate is a program developed by the U.S. Department of Agriculture designed to remind us how to eat healthfully. The focus is on foods to give you energy, keep you strong and make your body work smoothly.

The MyPlate illustration shows the five food groups that are building blocks for a healthy diet in a fun way for kids and other family members—it's a place setting for a meal. Before you eat, think about what goes on your plate or in your cup or bowl. On the next page are the food groups and what is included in each one.

So when you fill up your plate, have some fun with color and shape, but follow the guidelines for amounts. Make half of your plate fruits and vegetables with the other half divided into protein foods and grains. Be sure to make at least half of your grains whole grains.

Remember, your food and what you eat plus physical activity affect your health and how you feel—today, tomorrow and in the future.

Here are some tips to keep in mind every day.

- Make at least half of your grains whole grains—try a new grain occasionally.
- Vary your veggies—enjoy new textures and flavors.
- Focus on fruit for meals and snacks—they are colorful and taste good.
- Eat calcium-rich foods like milk and yogurt—try switching to fat-free or low-fat milk.
- Go lean with protein—avoid oversized portions.
- Drink water or 100% fruit juice instead of sugary drinks.

Favorite Fruits

Apples

Apricots

Bananas

Berries (strawberries, blueberries, raspberries)

Cherries

Grapes

Melons (cantaloupe, honeydew, watermelon)

Nectarines

Oranges and tangerines

Peaches

Pears

Pineapple

Raisins (and other dried fruit)

100% fruit juice (orange, grape, apple)

Vital Vegetables

Asparagus

Avocado

Beets

Broccoli

Brussels sprouts

Cabbage

Carrots

Cauliflower

Corn

Cucumbers

Dried beans/legumes (black beans, garbanzo beans, soybeans, black-eyed peas, lentils)

Greens (kale, spinach, dark green lettuce)

Green beans

Mushrooms

Peas

Potatoes

Squash (acorn, butternut, hubbard)

Sweet potatoes

Zucchini

Great Grains

Barley

Buckwheat

Bulgur

Oats (oatmeal)

Quinoa

Rice (white, brown, wild)

Wheat (bread, pasta, cereal)

Purely Protein

Eggs

Fish and seafood (salmon, tuna, shrimp)

Poultry (chicken, turkey)

Meats (beef, pork)

Nuts (peanuts, almonds, cashews, walnuts)

Beans and peas (black beans, split peas, lentils)

Seeds (sunflower, pumpkin)

Tofu

Dynamic Dairy

Cheese (cream, Cheddar, Swiss)

Cottage cheese and ricotta cheese

Milk

Yogurt

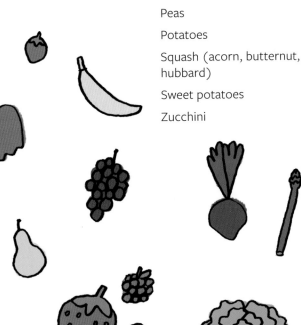

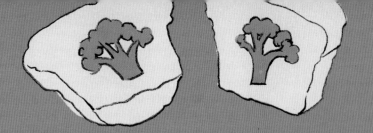

Breakfast

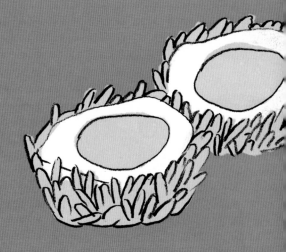

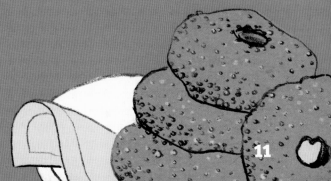

Blueberry Pie Muffins

Prep Time: 30 Minutes
Bake: 25 Minutes
Cool: 5 Minutes • 12 muffins

Filling

⅔	cup blueberry pie filling (from 21-ounce can)
⅓	cup fresh blueberries

Streusel

½	cup old-fashioned or quick-cooking oats
¼	cup all-purpose flour
¼	cup packed brown sugar
¼	teaspoon ground cinnamon
2	tablespoons cold butter, cut into small pieces

Muffins

1	lemon
¾	cup milk
¼	cup vegetable oil
1	egg
2	cups all-purpose flour
½	cup granulated sugar
2	teaspoons baking powder
½	teaspoon salt

For the prettiest muffins, drop the blueberry mixture near the center, allowing only some of it to go toward the edge of the muffin cup.

Adding fresh blueberries to the pie filling gives a burst of fresh fruit flavor. If blueberries are not in season, simply use 1 cup pie filling.

1 Muffin: Calories 230; Total Fat 8g (Saturated Fat 2.5g; Trans Fat 0g); Cholesterol 25mg; Sodium 210mg; Total Carbohydrate 37g (Dietary Fiber 1g); Protein 4g **Exchanges:** 1½ Starch, 1 Other Carbohydrate, 1½ Fat **Carbohydrate Choices:** 2½

1. Heat oven to 400°F. Line 12 regular-size muffin cups with paper baking cups, or use a brush or paper towel to grease the cups with shortening or cooking spray.

2. In small mixing bowl, mix filling ingredients with wooden spoon; set aside. In medium mixing bowl, mix all streusel ingredients with a fork until crumbly; set aside.

3. Use grater to grate 1 tablespoon peel from lemon. In large mixing bowl, beat milk, oil, egg and lemon peel with fork or whisk until blended. Stir in remaining muffin ingredients with wooden spoon all at once just until flour is moistened (batter will be lumpy).

4. Spoon about 1 tablespoon batter in bottom of each muffin cup (spread, if necessary, to cover most of bottom of cup). Alternately drop rounded ½ teaspoon blueberry mixture and 1 teaspoon remaining muffin batter in different areas in each muffin cup, layering as necessary. (Cups will be ¾ full.)

5. Sprinkle the streusel evenly over batter and blueberry mixture in each cup.

6. Bake 20 to 25 minutes or until golden brown and toothpick inserted in center of a muffin comes out clean. Use pot holders to remove the pan from the oven. Cool muffins 5 minutes in pan, then remove from pan to cooling rack. Serve warm if you like.

Utensils

- 12-cup muffin pan
- Paper baking cups
- Small mixing bowl
- Spoon
- Fork
- Wooden spoon
- Dry-ingredient measuring cups
- Liquid-ingredient measuring cups
- Medium mixing bowl
- Measuring spoons
- Whisk
- Grater
- Large mixing bowl
- Toothpicks
- Pot holders
- Cooling rack

13

For spicier muffins, substitute pepper Jack cheese for the Cheddar cheese.

Ask mom and dad to tuck these muffins into your lunch box as a great accompaniment to soup or chili.

14

Secret Forest Corn Muffins

Prep Time: 10 Minutes • **Bake: 18 Minutes**
Cool: 5 Minutes • **6 muffins**

1   **pouch cornbread and muffin mix**
     Milk
     Butter
1   **egg**
⅓   **cup shredded Cheddar cheese**
6   **frozen broccoli florets (from 12-ounce bag), thawed**

1. Heat oven to 350°F. Line 6 regular-size muffin cups with paper baking cups.

2. In medium mixing bowl, use a wooden spoon to stir muffin mix, milk, butter and egg as directed on the cornbread mix pouch (amounts will be on the pouch). Stir in ¼ cup of the cheese. (You will use the rest later.) Spoon about 1 tablespoon batter into each of the muffin cups. Place 1 broccoli floret in each muffin cup, stem side down, trimming stem if necessary so that floret fits in muffin cup. Spoon remaining batter over florets in muffin cups, covering completely.

3. Bake 15 minutes; sprinkle with the remaining cheese. Bake 1 to 3 minutes longer or until toothpick inserted in center of a muffin comes out clean. Use pot holders to remove the pan from the oven. Cool muffins 5 minutes in pan. Then remove from pan to cooling rack. Serve warm.

1 Muffin: Calories 200; Total Fat 8g (Saturated Fat 4g; Trans Fat 0g); Cholesterol 50mg; Sodium 300mg; Total Carbohydrate 25g (Dietary Fiber 0g); Protein 5g **Exchanges:** 1½ Starch, 1½ Fat **Carbohydrate Choices:** 1½

Utensils

- Muffin pan
- Wooden spoon
- Paper baking cups
- Medium mixing bowl
- Dry-ingredient measuring cups
- Measuring spoons
- Toothpicks
- Pot holders
- Cooling rack

Snickerdoodly Mini Doughnuts

Prep Time: 45 Minutes • **Bake:** 10 Minutes

Refrigerate: 1 Hour • **26 mini doughnuts**

Doughnuts

- ¼ cup butter
- ⅓ cup sugar
- 2 eggs
- ⅓ cup milk
- 3 tablespoons sour cream
- 1 teaspoon vanilla
- 2 cups all-purpose flour
- 1½ teaspoons ground cinnamon
- 1 teaspoon cream of tartar
- 1 teaspoon baking powder

Topping

- ¾ cup sugar
- 3 tablespoons ground cinnamon
- 6 tablespoons butter

Utensils

- Small microwavable bowl
- 2 medium mixing bowls
- Dry-ingredient measuring cups
- Liquid-ingredient measuring cups
- Measuring spoons
- Whisk
- Pastry brush
- Plastic wrap
- 2 cookie sheets
- Cooking parchment paper
- Rolling pin
- Round cutters
- Pancake turner
- Pot holders
- Cooling rack
- 2 small bowls
- 2 forks
- Spoon

1 👆 Place the ¼ cup butter in a small microwavable bowl; microwave on High 15 to 20 seconds or until melted. In medium mixing bowl, with whisk, mix ⅓ cup sugar, the melted butter and the eggs until smooth. Stir in milk, sour cream and vanilla. Stir in flour, 1½ teaspoons cinnamon, the cream of tartar and baking powder just until the mixture is moistened.

2 Using pastry brush or paper towel, grease medium mixing bowl with shortening. Place dough mixture in bowl. Cover bowl with plastic wrap; refrigerate 1 hour.

3 Heat oven to 450°F. Line 2 cookie sheets with cooking parchment paper. You will bake the doughnuts right on the parchment paper. Place dough on a counter or another surface generously sprinkled with flour. Roll dough in the flour to coat. With floured rolling pin, roll dough to ½-inch thickness. Cut dough with floured 1¾-inch round cookie cutter. Place the dough rounds on the parchment paper–lined cookie sheets about 1 inch apart. Cut out centers of the rounds using floured ¾-inch round cutter to make doughnut shapes. Reroll scraps and centers to cut additional doughnuts.

Refrigerating the dough makes it easier to roll, but extra flour is still needed to keep the dough from sticking to the counter and rolling pin. Shake off any excess flour before placing the dough rounds on the cookie sheet.

Cream of tartar adds the signature sweet-sour "snickerdoodle" taste to these doughnuts, distinguishing them from the regular cinnamon-sugar variety.

4 👆 Bake 8 to 10 minutes or until edges of the doughnuts just turn light golden brown. Use pot holders to remove cookie sheets from oven. With pancake turner, immediately remove doughnuts from cookie sheet and place on cooling rack. Cool 3 minutes.

5 In small bowl, stir together ¾ cup sugar and 3 tablespoons cinnamon. Using the microwavable bowl, microwave the 6 tablespoons butter 10 to 15 seconds or until melted. Using 2 forks, quickly dip both sides of each warm doughnut into butter; let excess drip off. Using spoon, roll each doughnut in cinnamon-sugar mixture to coat. Return doughnuts to cooling rack. Serve warm.

1 Mini Doughnut: Calories 120; Total Fat 5g (Saturated Fat 3g; Trans Fat 0g); Cholesterol 30mg; Sodium 60mg; Total Carbohydrate 17g (Dietary Fiber 1g); Protein 1g **Exchanges:** ½ Starch, ½ Other Carbohydrate, 1 Fat **Carbohydrate Choices:** 1

17

Bake 'Em Up Banana–Chocolate Chip Doughnuts

Prep Time: 25 Minutes • **Bake: 8 Minutes** • **16 doughnuts**

Doughnuts

- ½ cup butter, softened
- ⅔ cup granulated sugar
- 2 eggs
- 3 medium very ripe bananas
- 1 teaspoon vanilla
- 2¼ cups all-purpose flour
- 1½ teaspoons baking powder
- ½ teaspoon salt
- ½ cup miniature semisweet chocolate chips

Glaze

- 1 cup powdered sugar
- ½ cup caramel topping
- 4 to 5 teaspoons whipping cream

Garnish

Dried banana chips, chopped, if you like

1 Heat oven to 425°F. Lightly spray 2 regular-size doughnut pans (6 doughnuts per pan) with cooking spray.

2 In medium mixing bowl, beat butter, granulated sugar and eggs with electric mixer on medium speed until smooth. Place bananas in another mixing bowl; mash with fork until smooth (you will have about 1½ cups). Add bananas and vanilla to sugar mixture; beat on low speed until well mixed. Using wooden spoon, stir in flour, baking powder and salt just until flour is moistened. Stir in the chocolate chips.

3 Using 2 spoons, scoop batter evenly into doughnut pans, filling wells almost to the top. Bake 6 to 8 minutes or until toothpick inserted in the center of a doughnut comes out clean. Cool in pan 5 minutes; carefully remove doughnuts from pan and place on cooling rack.

4 While the doughnuts are cooling, in small mixing bowl, mix all glaze ingredients. Using a wooden spoon or rubber spatula, stir until well blended. Dip top of each doughnut into glaze or drizzle with glaze; sprinkle with the chopped banana chips. Place doughnuts on cooling rack or plate. Serve doughnuts warm or cool.

1 Doughnut: Calories 270; Total Fat 9g (Saturated Fat 5g; Trans Fat 0g); Cholesterol 40mg; Sodium 220mg; Total Carbohydrate 45g (Dietary Fiber 1g); Protein 3g **Exchanges:** 1 Starch, 2 Other Carbohydrate, 1½ Fat **Carbohydrate Choices:** 3

Miniature semisweet chocolate chips are the best choice because they won't sink in the batter and you get more chips in each bite!

Utensils

- 2 doughnut pans
- 2 medium mixing bowls
- Dry-ingredient measuring cups
- Liquid-ingredient measuring cups
- Electric mixer
- Measuring spoons
- Wooden spoon
- 2 spoons
- Toothpick
- Pot holders
- Cooling rack
- Small mixing bowl
- Sharp knife

Cranberry and Oat No-Knead Artisan Rolls

Prep Time: 40 Minutes • **Rise: 2 Hours** • **Refrigerate: 30 Minutes** • **Bake: 20 Minutes**
Cool: 5 Minutes • **16 rolls**

2   packages regular active yeast (2¼ teaspoons in each package)

1   tablespoon sugar

1½   cups warm water (105°F to 115°F)

¼   cup honey

2½   teaspoons vanilla

1   teaspoon salt

1   orange

½   teaspoon ground cinnamon

3½   to 4 cups white whole wheat flour

¾   cup quick-cooking oats

½   cup dried cranberries

2   tablespoons butter

Utensils

- Large mixing bowl
- Candy thermometer
- Grater
- Measuring spoons
- Liquid-ingredient measuring cup
- Dry-ingredient measuring cups
- Wooden spoon
- Plastic wrap
- Large cookie sheet
- Small microwavable bowl
- Pastry brush
- Pot holders
- Cooling rack

1 In large mixing bowl, sprinkle yeast and 1 tablespoon sugar over warm water; stir gently to dissolve. Let stand 10 minutes or until mixture is foamy.

2 Use grater to grate orange peel to measure 1 teaspoon. Add honey, vanilla, salt, orange peel and cinnamon; stir with wooden spoon until well mixed. Stir in flour, ½ cup of the oats and the cranberries until the mixture begins to pull away from side of bowl. Mixture will be sticky. Cover bowl loosely with plastic wrap and let rise in warm place about 2 hours or until dough is doubled in size. Refrigerate at least 30 minutes or up to 24 hours.

3 Spray large cookie sheet with cooking spray. On floured surface, divide dough evenly into 16 pieces. With floured hands, shape each piece into a ball by stretching surface of dough around to bottom on all 4 sides; pinch bottom to seal. Place 2 inches apart on cookie sheet.

4 Heat oven to 375°F. Cover rolls loosely with plastic wrap and let stand 30 minutes at room temperature. In small microwavable bowl, microwave butter on High 10 to 15 seconds or until melted. Lightly brush tops of rolls with melted butter; sprinkle evenly with the remaining ¼ cup oats.

5 Bake 15 to 20 minutes or until rolls are deep golden brown and bread sounds hollow when tapped. Remove from cookie sheet to cooling rack; cool 5 minutes. Serve warm or cool.

1 Roll: Calories 160; Total Fat 2.5g (Saturated Fat 1g; Trans Fat 0g); Cholesterol 0mg; Sodium 160mg; Total Carbohydrate 30g (Dietary Fiber 3g); Protein 4g **Exchanges:** 1½ Starch, ½ Other Carbohydrate, ½ Fat **Carbohydrate Choices:** 2

After you grate the amount of orange peel for the recipe, you can eat the orange!

Coarsely shredding frozen butter is an easy way to disperse small butter pieces into biscuit dough, giving tender-flaky results.

Super-Tasty Sweet Potato–Bacon Biscuits

Prep Time: 20 Minutes • Bake: 15 Minutes

8 biscuits

- 1½ cups all-purpose flour
- 3 teaspoons baking powder
- ¼ teaspoon salt
- 8 slices bacon, crisply cooked**, crumbled
- ½ teaspoon chopped fresh thyme leaves
- ¼ cup butter, frozen
- ⅔ cup sweet potatoes (from 15-ounce can)
- 2 tablespoons buttermilk
- 2 tablespoons butter

1 Heat oven to 450°F. In large mixing bowl, combine flour, baking powder and salt; stir with wooden spoon. Stir in bacon and thyme. Shred frozen butter, using large holes of grater; add to flour mixture and toss to coat. Place a few pieces of sweet potato into a small bowl. Using fork, mash until you can measure ⅔ cup. Stir sweet potatoes and buttermilk into flour mixture with wooden spoon just until soft dough forms.

2 Place dough on lightly floured surface; gently roll in flour to coat. Knead lightly 4 or 5 times. Press dough or roll with rolling pin to ¾-inch thickness. Cut with floured 2½-inch biscuit cutter. On ungreased cookie sheet, place biscuits about 1 inch apart.

3 Bake 12 to 15 minutes or until light golden brown. Use pot holders to remove cookie sheet from oven. Place butter in small microwavable bowl. Microwave on High 10 to 15 seconds or until melted. Brush warm rolls with melted butter. Serve warm.

1 Biscuit: Calories 180; Total Fat 7g (Saturated Fat 3g; Trans Fat 0g); Cholesterol 15mg; Sodium 480mg; Total Carbohydrate 24g (Dietary Fiber 1g); Protein 6g **Exchanges:** 1½ Starch, 1½ Fat **Carbohydrate Choices:** 1½

Utensils

- Large mixing bowl
- Dry-ingredient measuring cups
- Measuring spoons
- Wooden spoon
- Grater
- Ruler
- Biscuit cutter
- Cookie sheet
- Pastry brush
- Rolling pin
- Pot holders
- Small microwavable bowl
- Cooling rack

**Usually you can purchase cooked bacon. Then all you need to do is crumble it. But if you have bacon that is not cooked, have an adult help you to cook it.

Cinnamon Bubble Loaf

Prep Time: 15 Minutes • **Bake: 30 Minutes**

Stand: 10 Minutes • **1 loaf (12 slices)**

Loaf

2	tablespoons granulated sugar
1½	teaspoons ground cinnamon
3½	cups all-purpose buttermilk baking mix
⅓	cup granulated sugar

3	tablespoons butter, softened
½	cup milk
1	teaspoon vanilla
1	egg
2	tablespoons butter

Glaze

½	cup powdered sugar
2	to 3 teaspoons water

1. Heat oven to 375°F. Using pastry brush or paper towel, grease bottom and sides of 9×5-inch loaf pan with shortening or spray with cooking spray. In small mixing bowl, mix 2 tablespoons granulated sugar and the cinnamon; set aside.

2. In medium mixing bowl, combine baking mix, ⅓ cup granulated sugar, 3 tablespoons softened butter, the milk, vanilla and egg; stir with wooden spoon until soft dough forms.

3. Using your hands, shape dough into 1-inch balls; roll in cinnamon-sugar. Place dough balls randomly in pan. Sprinkle with any remaining cinnamon-sugar. Place 2 tablespoons butter in small microwavable bowl. Microwave on High 10 to 15 seconds or until melted. Drizzle butter over dough balls.

4. Bake 25 to 30 minutes or until golden brown. Use pot holders to remove pan from oven. Let stand in pan 10 minutes. Meanwhile, in small mixing bowl, mix glaze ingredients with wooden spoon until smooth and thin enough to drizzle.

5. Remove loaf from pan to cooling rack. With spoon, drizzle glaze over loaf.

Cut into slices. Serve warm.

1 Slice: Calories 250; Total Fat 10g (Saturated Fat 4.5g; Trans Fat 1.5g); Cholesterol 30mg; Sodium 470mg; Total Carbohydrate 36g (Dietary Fiber 1g); Protein 3g **Exchanges:** 1½ Starch, 1 Other Carbohydrate, 2 Fat **Carbohydrate Choices:** 2½

Utensils

- Pastry brush
- 9×5-inch loaf pan
- 2 small mixing bowls
- Measuring spoons
- Medium mixing bowl
- Dry-ingredient measuring cups
- Liquid-ingredient measuring cups
- Wooden spoon
- Pot holders
- Small microwavable bowl
- Cooling rack

Cinnamon-Raisin French Toast

Prep Time: 5 Minutes • **Cook: 16 Minutes** • **4 servings (2 slices French toast each)**

2	eggs
1	egg white
¾	cup milk
1	tablespoon sugar
½	teaspoon vanilla
8	slices cinnamon-raisin bread

1 In small mixing bowl, beat eggs, milk, sugar and vanilla with whisk or hand beater until smooth; pour into shallow bowl.

2 Spray griddle or 10-inch skillet with cooking spray; heat griddle to 375°F or heat skillet over medium heat. Dip bread into egg mixture, turning to coat both sides.

3 Cook about 4 minutes; turn with pancake turner. Cook about 4 minutes on other side or until golden brown.

1 Serving: Calories 210; Total Fat 5g (Saturated Fat 1g; Trans Fat 0g); Cholesterol 110mg; Sodium 270mg; Total Carbohydrate 33g (Dietary Fiber 2g); Protein 10g **Exchanges:** 2 Starch, 1 Lean Meat **Carbohydrate Choices:** 2

Utensils

- Small mixing bowl
- Liquid-ingredient measuring cups
- Measuring spoons
- Whisk or hand beater
- Shallow bowl
- Griddle or 10-inch skillet
- Pancake turner

Silver Dollar Bacon Waffles with Peach-Raspberry Sauce

Prep Time: 15 Minutes • **Cool: 15 Minutes** • **Bake: 10 Minutes**

11 servings (4 waffles and 1½ tablespoons sauce each)

1	(15-ounce) can peaches in peach juice
1	(10-ounce) jar raspberry preserves (about 1 cup)
1¼	cups buttermilk baking mix
¾	cup milk
1	egg
1	tablespoon vegetable oil
3	slices bacon, crisply cooked, crumbled**

1 Place peaches in colander over small bowl; let stand for 2 to 3 minutes or until drained. Place 3 tablespoons peach juice in 1-quart saucepan. Add raspberry preserves.

Cook over medium-low heat, stirring frequently with wooden spoon, 1 to 2 minutes or until mixture comes to a boil. Boil 1 minute. Remove from heat. Cool 15 minutes.

2 Heat nonstick Belgian waffle maker or regular waffle maker. Using pastry brush, grease with shortening or vegetable oil. In large mixing bowl, stir baking mix, milk, egg, oil and bacon with wooden spoon until blended. Spoon 1 teaspoon batter onto each square or section of waffle maker. Close lid of waffle maker.

3 Bake 1 to 1½ minutes or until steam stops. Carefully remove waffles with a fork. Repeat with remaining batter. Keep waffles warm on a plate covered with foil.

4 With table knife, cut each peach slice in half lengthwise. To serve place 4 waffles on each serving plate, top with 2 peach slices. Drizzle with raspberry-peach sauce.

1 Serving: Calories 190; Total Fat 5g (Saturated Fat 1.5g; Trans Fat 0g); Cholesterol 20mg; Sodium 240mg; Total Carbohydrate 32g (Dietary Fiber 1g); Protein 3g **Exchanges:** 1 Starch, 1 Other Carbohydrate, 1 Fat **Carbohydrate Choices:** 2

To freeze and then reheat the waffles, stack cooled waffles between waxed paper. Wrap in foil and freeze. To reheat in oven, unwrap waffles; remove waxed paper. Heat on ungreased cookie sheet in 400°F oven 5 to 8 minutes or until hot.

**Usually you can purchase cooked bacon. Then all you need to do is crumble it. But if you have bacon that is not cooked, have an adult help you to cook it.

Utensils

- Can opener
- Colander
- Small bowl
- Measuring spoons
- 1-quart saucepan
- Wooden spoon
- Belgian or regular waffle maker
- Pastry brush
- Measuring spoons
- Large mixing bowl
- Dry-ingredient measuring cups
- Liquid-ingredient measuring cups
- Fork
- Table knife
- Plates

Apple Crisp Refrigerator Oatmeal

Prep Time: 10 Minutes • Refrigerate: 8 Hours • 1 serving

Oatmeal

- ¼ cup old-fashioned oats
- 1 container (6 ounces) apple crisp low-fat yogurt
- 1 teaspoon chia seed, if you like

Toppings, if you like

- 1 Granny Smith apple
- ⅛ teaspoon ground cinnamon
- 2 tablespoons chopped walnuts

Utensils

- Half-pint canning jar
- Dry-ingredient measuring cups
- Measuring spoons
- Spoon
- Sharp knife
- Cutting board

1 In half-pint canning jar (or other resealable container), combine oats and yogurt. Top with chia seed; carefully stir with spoon to mix thoroughly. Cover; refrigerate about 8 hours.

2 When ready to serve, place apple on cutting board.

With sharp knife, chop apple into small pieces (you can leave the peel on) to measure ¼ cup. Sprinkle apple, cinnamon and walnuts over oatmeal.

1 Serving: Calories 240; Total Fat 3g (Saturated Fat 1g; Trans Fat 0g); Cholesterol 10mg; Sodium 90mg; Total Carbohydrate 47g (Dietary Fiber 2g); Protein 7g **Exchanges:** 1½ Starch, 1½ Other Carbohydrate, ½ Fat **Carbohydrate Choices:** 3

Chia seed is a delicious addition to this dish and it helps to thicken dishes. Chia seed is good in smoothies, too.

You only need part of the apple for the oatmeal. After you chop what you need for the recipe, you can eat the rest!

Bowls of Quinoa Treasure

Prep Time: 5 Minutes • Cook: 15 Minutes

4 servings (½ cup each)

1	cup uncooked quinoa
2	cups water, milk or soymilk
¼	teaspoon ground cinnamon
1	cup fresh or frozen (thawed) blueberries
¼	cup pecans or walnuts, toasted, if you like**
	Maple syrup, if you like

Utensils

- Dry-ingredient measuring cups
- Fine mesh strainer
- 1-quart saucepan
- Liquid-ingredient measuring cups
- Measuring spoons
- Wooden spoon
- Bowls

**To toast pecans, place on shallow pan. Bake at 350°F 10 to 12 minutes or until golden brown, stirring occasionally.

Use more liquid for a creamier cereal, or you can serve additional milk or cream on the side.

1 Rinse quinoa thoroughly by placing in a fine mesh strainer and holding under cold running water until water runs clear; drain well.

2 In 1-quart saucepan, heat water and quinoa to boiling. Reduce heat to low; cover and simmer 15 minutes or until liquid is absorbed (mixture will still be moist).

3 Stir in cinnamon with wooden spoon. Spoon quinoa into bowls. Top with blueberries and pecans. Sweeten to taste with a drizzle of maple syrup.

1 Serving: Calories 230; Total Fat 7g (Saturated Fat 0.5g; Trans Fat 0g); Cholesterol 0mg; Sodium 5mg; Total Carbohydrate 34g (Dietary Fiber 4g); Protein 7g **Exchanges:** 2½ Starch, 1 Fat **Carbohydrate Choices:** 2

Rise and Shine Kabobs with Yogurt Dip

Prep Time: 25 Minutes • 4 servings (2 kabobs and 2 tablespoons dip each)

4   ounces Muenster cheese

½   medium cantaloupe (You
     need about 2 cups cubed)

1   cup fresh strawberries

4   slices (½ inch thick)
     French bread

2   ounces thinly sliced hard
     salami, folded into quarters

1   cup creamy harvest
     peach, creamy strawberry
     or creamy strawberry-
     banana yogurt

BEEP! BEEP! BEEP!

6:00

Robo-Guy

1 On cutting board, use sharp knife to cut cheese into small cubes. Then cut rind from cantaloupe and cut yellow part into cubes too. Cut the strawberries in half and the French bread into cubes. Onto wooden skewers, thread salami, cheese, fruit and bread.

2 Place yogurt in small bowl. Serve kabobs with yogurt as a dip.

1 Serving: Calories 330; Total Fat 15g (Saturated Fat 8g; Trans Fat 0g); Cholesterol 40mg; Sodium 630mg; Total Carbohydrate 34g (Dietary Fiber 2g); Protein 15g **Exchanges:** 1½ Starch, 1 Fruit, 2½ Other Carbohydrate, 1½ High-Fat Meat **Carbohydrate Choices:**

Utensils

- Cutting board
- Sharp knife
- 8 wooden skewers (8 inch)
- Dry-ingredient measuring cups
- Small bowl

Thread the kabobs the night before, leaving a little space between each ingredient. Cover tightly and refrigerate until you are ready to serve them.

Veggie-licious Omelet

Prep Time: 10 Minutes • **Cook: 12 Minutes** • **2 servings (½ omelet each)**

Filling

- 1 small zucchini
- ½ small onion
- ¼ medium red bell pepper
- ¼ medium yellow or green bell pepper
- ¼ cup sliced fresh mushrooms
- ¼ teaspoon salt
- Dash pepper

Omelet

- 4 eggs
- 1 tablespoon milk

Toppings

- ¼ cup shredded Swiss cheese
- 1 small plum (Roma) tomato

Utensils

- Cutting board
- Sharp knife
- Dry-ingredient measuring cups
- Measuring spoons
- 8- to 10-inch nonstick skillet
- Plate
- Paper towel
- Small mixing bowl
- Whisk
- Rubber spatula
- Wide spatula

1 Place zucchini on cutting board. Cut into ¼-inch-thick slices using sharp knife; cut each slice into quarters (you need ¼ cup). Slice the onion to measure ¼ cup. Chop the bell peppers into small pieces to measure ½ cup total.

2 Heat 8- to 10-inch nonstick skillet with sloping sides (omelet pan) over medium heat. Add zucchini and remaining filling ingredients; cook 4 to 6 minutes, stirring occasionally, until tender. Remove cooked vegetables from skillet; place on plate and cover to keep warm. Cool skillet 1 minute; carefully wipe clean with paper towel.

3 In small mixing bowl, beat eggs and milk using whisk or fork. Heat same skillet over medium heat. Pour egg mixture into skillet; cook 4 to 5 minutes without stirring, but lifting edges occasionally with rubber spatula to allow uncooked egg mixture to flow to bottom of skillet, until mixture is set but top is still moist.

4 On cutting board, cut tomato into a few slices with sharp knife. Spoon cooked vegetables onto half of omelet; sprinkle with cheese. Loosen edge of omelet using wide spatula and fold over vegetables. Arrange tomato slices on top of omelet.

1 Serving: Calories 120; Total Fat 1g (Saturated Fat 0.5g; Trans Fat 0g); Cholesterol 5mg; Sodium 550mg; Total Carbohydrate 9g (Dietary Fiber 2g); Protein 17g **Exchanges:** 1½ Vegetable, 2 Very Lean Meat **Carbohydrate Choices:** ½

This is a great way to include veggies in the morning. The red, yellow and green bell peppers are high in vitamin C, and all the vegetables contain some fiber.

We like the Swiss cheese, but if your family prefers mozzarella, Cheddar or Colby, don't be afraid to choose one of those cheeses instead. They are all delicious.

37

Wake Up to an Omelet

Breakfast—it seems like creativity in the morning is not always easy to achieve. But because many feel it is the most important meal of the day, why not try whipping up an omelet? It's easy, fun and will wake up those taste buds with an old favorite. Add one or two fillings from the choices below and make your omelet extra yummy!

For each omelet, place 2 eggs in a medium bowl with just a sprinkle of salt and pepper; beat with a whisk or fork until fluffy. Heat an 8-inch nonstick skillet with sloping sides (omelet pan) over medium heat and add 2 teaspoons butter. When it is melted, pour in the egg mixture, turning the pan to make sure that it coats the bottom. Cook 3 to 5 minutes or until the bottom is brown and the egg is cooked through. Use a rubber spatula to lift the edges while the omelet cooks so that some egg mixture can flow to the bottom. When it is cooked, use the spatula to carefully flip one side over the other to make a half-moon shape and slide it onto a plate.

Before flipping, try adding one or two of these fillings:

- Shredded cheese (2 to 4 tablespoons)
- Chopped tomato (¼ cup)
- Chopped cooked ham (¼ cup)
- Crumbled cooked bacon (2 to 4 tablespoons)
- Sliced avocado (2 or 3 slices)
- Chopped fresh herbs like basil, chives or parsley (2 to 3 teaspoons)
- Chunky-style salsa (2 tablespoons)

Egg-Topped Hash Brown Nests

Prep Time: 20 Minutes
Bake: 35 Minutes • Cool: 5 Minutes
6 servings (2 egg nests each)

1	box (5.2 oz) seasoned hash brown potatoes
	Hot water
	Salt
	Butter
¼	cup bacon flavor bits or chips, if you like
12	eggs
1	teaspoon salt
½	teaspoon pepper

1 Heat oven to 400°F. Spray 12 regular-size muffin cups with cooking spray.

2 Make potatoes as directed on box using hot water, salt and butter (amounts will be on the box). When done, place in medium mixing bowl. Stir in bacon bits with wooden spoon. Spoon mixture evenly into muffin cups, dividing evenly.

Bake about 15 minutes or until potatoes start to turn golden brown on edges. Use pot holders to remove pan from oven. Reduce oven temperature to 350°F.

3 Carefully break 1 egg over each muffin cup. Sprinkle egg with salt and pepper. Bake 18 to 20 minutes or until egg whites and yolks are firm, not runny. Cool 5 minutes before removing from muffin cups.

1 Serving: Calories 280; Total Fat 16g (Saturated Fat 4g; Trans Fat 0.5g); Cholesterol 425mg; Sodium 770mg; Total Carbohydrate 20g (Dietary Fiber 2g); Protein 14g **Exchanges:** 1½ Starch, 1½ Medium-Fat Meat, 1½ Fat **Carbohydrate Choices:** 1

Make this a complete breakfast by adding some fresh fruit on the side for a burst of sweetness and color—Yum!

Utensils

- 12-cup muffin cup pan
- Pan for potatoes
- Medium mixing bowl
- Wooden spoon
- Dry-ingredient measuring cups
- Liquid-ingredient measuring cups
- Measuring spoons
- Pot holders
- Cooling rack

Lunch

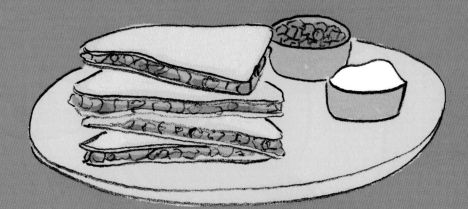

Spook-tacular Chocolate-Almond Spread

Prep Time: 10 Minutes • **16 servings (1 tablespoon each)**

½ cup semisweet chocolate chips

2 cups roasted unsalted whole almonds (½ pound)

1 teaspoon sugar

¼ teaspoon vanilla

¼ teaspoon sea salt

Utensils

- Small microwavable bowl
- Spoon
- Food processor
- Dry-ingredient measuring cups
- Measuring spoons
- Rubber spatula

1 Place chocolate chips in small microwavable bowl. Microwave on High 30 to 40 seconds or until melted, stirring with spoon every 20 seconds. Let stand until cooled, about 10 minutes.

2 In food processor, place melted chocolate chips and all remaining ingredients. Cover and process 2 to 4 minutes, scraping bowl with rubber spatula occasionally until smooth (do not over process). Store covered in refrigerator up to 1 month.

1 Serving: Calories 130; Total Fat 10g (Saturated Fat 1g; Trans Fat 0g); Cholesterol 0mg; Sodium 35mg; Total Carbohydrate 6g (Dietary Fiber 2g); Protein 3g **Exchanges:** ½ Other Carbohydrate, ½ Very Lean Meat, 2 Fat **Carbohydrate Choices:** ½

Honey-Cashew Spread Place 2 cups salted roasted cashews, ⅓ cup vegetable oil and 2 tablespoons honey in food processor. Cover and process 2 to 5 minutes or until smooth (do not over process).

Serve this delicious nut spread as a snack with sliced apples or bananas or on bagels or toast.

Wild West Vegetable Wraps

Prep Time: 15 Minutes • **8 servings (½ wrap each)**

1 large tomato
1 medium carrot
1 small yellow bell pepper
4 ounces (half of 8-ounce package) cream cheese, softened

4 flour tortillas (9 or 10 inch)
1 cup loosely packed fresh spinach
8 slices (1 ounce each) Muenster or Monterey Jack cheese

1 Place tomato on cutting board; use sharp knife to slice thinly. Using grater, grate carrot to measure ¾ cup. Chop bell pepper to measure ½ cup.

2 Spread 2 tablespoons of the cream cheese over each tortilla using table knife. Place spinach and tomato over tortillas leaving about a 1 inch border around the edges. Sprinkle with carrot. Top with cheese slices. Sprinkle with bell pepper.

3 Roll up tortillas with filling inside. Serve right away, or wrap tightly with plastic wrap and refrigerate up to 24 hours.

Utensils

- Cutting board
- Sharp knife
- Grater
- Measuring spoons
- Table knife
- Dry-ingredient measuring cups
- Grater

1 Serving: Calories 480; Total Fat 30g (Saturated Fat 18g; Trans Fat 1g); Cholesterol 85mg; Sodium 670mg; Total Carbohydrate 31g (Dietary Fiber 3g); Protein 20g **Exchanges:** 2 Starch, 2 High-Fat Meat, 2 Fat **Carbohydrate Choices:** 2

Customize your sandwich wrap by experimenting with flavored cream cheese, cooked frozen edamame, chopped fresh broccoli, sliced green onions or shredded zucchini. Or add your favorite cheeses and deli meats as you like.

Hummus is a delicious substitute for the cream cheese.

Super-Duper Sandwiches

It's a tall order to come up with sandwiches for lunch boxes or eating at home that are made with favorite foods—and are good for you. With the following list of choices, kids and other family members can stack up their favorite ingredients to make great sandwiches. And because you make your own, there will be no complaints!

Change up the bread—try whole wheat slices, pumpernickel slices, pita pockets, pita folds, tortillas, French bread slices or buns of any size or type. Just for fun, use a cookie cutter to cut shapes from bread slices. Then mix 'n match and stack it up!

Foods to Layer

Cheese slices

Meat slices

Tomato slices

Lettuce leaves

Cucumber slices

Pickles

Avocado slices

Peanut butter

Jelly or jam

Hummus

Mayonnaise

Fun to Try

Banana slices

Raisins or other dried fruit

Mustard

Spinach leaves

Cream cheese

Kale leaves

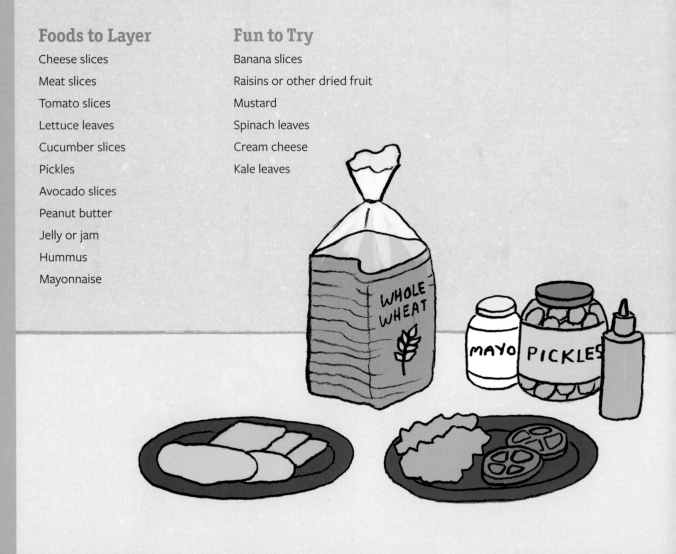

Awesome Avocado Toast

Prep Time: 15 Minutes • 2 servings

2 slices whole-grain or white Artisan bread (¼-inch slices), toasted
½ large avocado
¼ cup mayonnaise or salad dressing
½ teaspoon lemon juice
⅛ teaspoon sea salt
1 small plum (Roma) tomato
1 slice cooked bacon, crumbled**

1 With small spoon, scoop the pit out of the avocado half; remove peel with fingers. In small mixing bowl, mash avocado with fork. Stir in mayonnaise, lemon juice and sea salt until well blended.

2 Using table knife spread about 2 tablespoons avocado mixture onto each toast slice.

Place tomato on cutting board. Cut in half; scoop out seeds with spoon. Chop into small pieces using sharp knife. Top avocado mixture with tomato and bacon. Serve immediately.

1 Serving: Calories 350; Total Fat 29g (Saturated Fat 4.5g; Trans Fat 0g); Cholesterol 15mg; Sodium 530mg; Total Carbohydrate 17g (Dietary Fiber 5g); Protein 5g **Exchanges:** 1 Starch, ½ Medium-Fat Meat, 5 Fat **Carbohydrate Choices:** 1

Avocado Pesto Toast Omit mayonnaise, tomato and bacon. Stir 1 teaspoon prepared pesto into mashed avocado; spread on toast slices. Sprinkle with 2 teaspoons shredded parmesan cheese.

Utensils

- Cutting board
- Small spoon
- Sharp knife
- Small mixing bowl
- Fork
- Dry-ingredient measuring cups
- Table knife
- Measuring spoons

**Usually you can purchase cooked bacon. Then all you need to do is crumble it. But if you have bacon that is not cooked, have an adult help you to cook it.

AWESOME

Tug-of-War Grilled Cheesy Sandwiches

Prep Time: 10 Minutes • Cook: 8 Minutes • 4 sandwiches

8   slices white or whole wheat bread

12 slices American cheese (about ½ pound) or 2 cups shredded Cheddar cheese

⅓   cup butter, softened

Utensils

- Table knife
- Measuring teaspoon
- 12-inch skillet
- Spatula

1 Place 4 bread slices on clean counter. Top each slice with 3 slices cheese or ½ cup shredded cheese. Top with remaining bread slices. Spread 2 teaspoons butter over each top slice of bread.

2 Place sandwiches, buttered side down, in 12-inch skillet. Using table knife, spread remaining butter over top slices of bread.

Cook uncovered over medium-low heat about 5 minutes or until bottoms of sandwiches are golden brown. Turn carefully, using spatula; cook 2 to 3 minutes or until golden brown on both sides and cheese is melted.

1 Sandwich: Calories 480; Total Fat 35g (Saturated Fat 19g; Trans Fat 1.5g); Cholesterol 95mg; Sodium 1180mg; Total Carbohydrate 26g (Dietary Fiber 0g); Protein 17g **Exchanges:** 2 Starch, 2 High-Fat Meat, 2½ Fat **Carbohydrate Choices:** 2

Bacon, Tomato and Avocado Grilled Cheese Sandwiches

Place ¼ cup shredded cheese on each of 4 bread slices. Divide among 4 sandwiches ⅓ cup chopped onion, 8 slices cooked bacon, 1 medium tomato, thinly sliced, and 1 medium avocado, thinly sliced. Top with remaining cheese and bread. Spread butter over top slices of bread. Continue as directed in step 2.

Pesto-Parmesan Grilled Cheese

Spread purchased basil pesto lightly over each bread slice before adding cheese in step 1. Sprinkle butter-topped slices with Parmesan cheese before grilling.

Use any other type of shredded or sliced cheese that you like. Monterey Jack, Swiss, Gruyère, Jarlsberg or Gouda are all good choices.

53

After-the-Hike Tuna Melts

Prep Time: 10 Minutes • Broil: 5 Minutes • 4 sandwiches

- 4 slices whole-grain bread
- 2 cans (5 ounces each) chunk albacore (white) tuna in water, drained
- 1 can (8 ounces) crushed pineapple in juice, well drained (½ cup)
- ¼ cup mayonnaise or salad dressing
- ¼ small red onion

- 1 sprig fresh tarragon or ½ teaspoon dried tarragon leaves
- 1 large or 2 small plum (Roma) tomatoes
- 4 slices (¾ ounce each) Swiss cheese

1. Set oven control to broil. Place bread slices on a cookie sheet.

👍 Broil with tops of the bread about 5 inches from heat for 1 to 2 minutes per side, or until lightly toasted; set aside.

2. In medium mixing bowl, combine tuna, pineapple and mayonnaise just until mixed.

🔪 Place onion on cutting board; chop finely with sharp knife to measure 2 tablespoons. Chop tarragon to measure ½ teaspoon. Add onion and tarragon to tuna mixture; mix well with spoon. Spread tuna evenly on toasted bread slices. Place tomato on cutting board; cut into 8 thin slices. Top each sandwich with 2 tomato slices and 1 cheese slice.

3. Broil 3 to 5 minutes or until cheese is melted and sandwiches are hot. Cool slightly as cheese will be hot.

1 Sandwich: Calories 300; Total Fat 13g (Saturated Fat 5g; Trans Fat 0g); Cholesterol 40mg; Sodium 460mg; Total Carbohydrate 23g (Dietary Fiber 3g); Protein 24g **Exchanges:** ½ Starch, 1 Other Carbohydrate, ½ Vegetable, 2½ Very Lean Meat, ½ High-Fat Meat, 1½ Fat **Carbohydrate Choices:** 1½

Utensils

- Cookie sheet
- Ruler
- Cutting board
- Sharp knife
- Pot holders
- Cooling rack
- Can opener
- Dry-ingredient measuring cups
- Measuring spoons

To prevent corners and edges of the toasted bread slices from getting too dark when broiling, make sure to spread the tuna mixture to the edges.

Game-Time Quesadilla Wedges

Prep Time: 20 Minutes • **8 servings (½ quesadilla each)**

½ pound bacon

8 flour tortillas (7 or 8 inch)

1 cup canned refried beans

2 cups shredded Mexican cheese blend

2 medium green onions, chopped

Butter, melted

1 cup sour cream

1 cup salsa

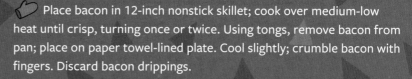

1 Place bacon in 12-inch nonstick skillet; cook over medium-low heat until crisp, turning once or twice. Using tongs, remove bacon from pan; place on paper towel-lined plate. Cool slightly; crumble bacon with fingers. Discard bacon drippings.

2 Spread half of each tortilla with beans using the back of a spoon. Sprinkle each with cheese, bacon and green onion. Fold unfilled half of tortilla over filling; press down with back of pancake turner. Lightly brush melted butter on both sides of each filled tortilla.

3 Heat 12-inch nonstick skillet over medium heat. (If using same skillet as above, clean before cooking quesadillas.) Cook 2 filled tortillas at a time 3 to 4 minutes, turning once, until golden brown and heated through.

Cut into wedges with pizza cutter or sharp knife. Serve with sour cream and salsa.

1 Serving: Calories 390; Total Fat 24g (Saturated Fat 13g; Trans Fat 1.5g); Cholesterol 60mg; Sodium 1070mg; Total Carbohydrate 28g (Dietary Fiber 1g); Protein 14g **Exchanges:** 1½ Starch, ½ Other Carbohydrate, ½ Medium-Fat Meat, 1 High-Fat Meat, 2½ Fat **Carbohydrate Choices:** 2

Utensils

- 12-inch nonstick skillet
- Tongs
- Paper towels
- Plate
- Can opener
- Dry-ingredient measuring cups
- Spoon
- Pancake turner
- Pastry brush
- Pizza cutter or sharp knife

This is the perfect recipe to make with leftover bacon from breakfast. Simply crumble up the cooked slices and you're ready to go!

Family-Fun Pizzettes

Prep Time: 5 Minutes • Bake: 10 Minutes
16 servings (1 English muffin half each)

8   English muffins, split, toasted
1   cup pizza sauce
2   cups shredded provolone cheese
    Assorted toppings (⅔ cup each sliced mushrooms, sliced ripe olives, chopped bell pepper and chopped red onion)

1 Heat oven to 425°F.
With fingers, carefully split each English muffin in half. Toast in toaster or toaster oven. Spoon and spread 1 tablespoon pizza sauce over each English muffin half. Sprinkle each with 1 tablespoon of the cheese. Arrange about ⅓ cup toppings on each pizza. Sprinkle with remaining cheese.

2 Place on ungreased cookie sheet. Bake 5 to 10 minutes or until cheese is melted. Cool slightly as cheese will be very hot.

1 Serving: Calories 130; Total Fat 6g (Saturated Fat 2.5g; Trans Fat 0g); Cholesterol 10mg; Sodium 370mg; Total Carbohydrate 16g (Dietary Fiber 1g); Protein 6g **Exchanges:** 1 Starch, ½ High-Fat Meat **Carbohydrate Choices:** 1

Utensils

- Toaster
- Liquid-ingredient measuring cup
- Measuring spoons
- Dry-ingredient measuring cups
- Cookie sheet
- Pot holders
- Cooling rack

Try mozzarella in place of the provolone cheese, if you like.

59

Surprise! Confetti Pasta Salad

Prep Time: 10 Minutes • **Cook: 12 Minutes** • **8 servings (¾ cup each)**

8   ounces uncooked bow-tie (farfalle) pasta

2   cups frozen mixed vegetables

½   small red onion

1   medium tomato

½   cup reduced-fat Italian dressing

Utensils

- 2-quart saucepan
- Dry-ingredient measuring cups
- Cutting board
- Sharp knife
- Colander
- Medium mixing bowl
- Spoon
- Liquid-ingredient measuring cup

1   Cook pasta as directed on package, adding the frozen mixed vegetables during the last 5 to 7 minutes of cooking time. Cook until the vegetables are tender. Drain in colander; rinse pasta and vegetables with cold water. Drain well.

2   Place onion on cutting board; chop into small pieces with sharp knife to measure ¼ cup. Chop tomato. In medium mixing bowl, gently stir cooled cooked pasta and vegetables with onion, tomato and dressing. Serve right away, or cover and refrigerate until serving time.

1 Serving: Calories 150; Total Fat 3.5g (Saturated Fat 0.5g; Trans Fat 0g); Cholesterol 0mg; Sodium 200mg; Total Carbohydrate 25g (Dietary Fiber 2g); Protein 4g **Exchanges:** 1½ Starch, ½ Vegetable, ½ Fat **Carbohydrate Choices:** 1½

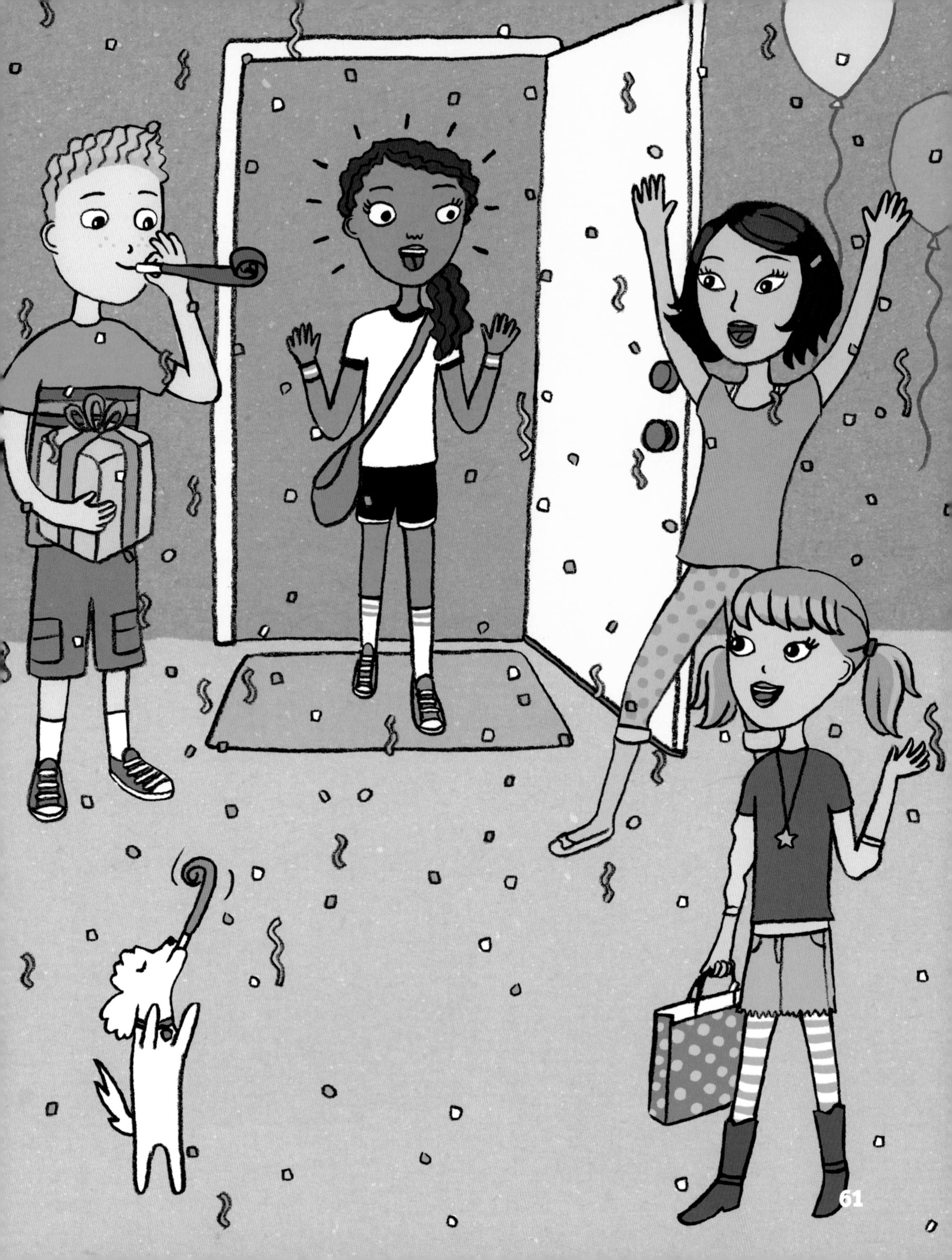

Lunch-Time A-B-C Soup

Prep Time: 5 Minutes • **Cook: 15 Minutes** • **10 servings (1¼ cups each)**

1   small rib celery
½   small onion
2   cups cubed cooked chicken or turkey

2   cups frozen mixed vegetables
¼   teaspoon dried thyme leaves
1   bay leaf

6   cups reduced-sodium chicken broth (from two 32-ounce cartons)
1   cup uncooked alphabet macaroni

1 Place celery and onion on cutting board. Chop each vegetable into small pieces with sharp knife to measure ½ cup chopped celery and ¼ cup chopped onion.

2 In 4-quart saucepan, mix all ingredients except macaroni. Heat to boiling, stirring occasionally with wooden spoon. Reduce heat; stir in macaroni.

3 Simmer 12 to 15 minutes or until vegetables and macaroni are tender. Remove bay leaf. If you like, sprinkle with a little salt and pepper.

1 Serving: Calories 140; Total Fat 2.5g (Saturated Fat 0.5g; Trans Fat 0g); Cholesterol 25mg; Sodium 370mg; Total Carbohydrate 17g (Dietary Fiber 2g); Protein 13g **Exchanges:** 1 Starch, ½ Vegetable, 1 Lean Meat **Carbohydrate Choices:** 1

Utensils

- Cutting board
- Sharp knife
- 4-quart saucepan
- Dry-ingredient measuring cups
- Measuring spoons
- Liquid-ingredient measuring cup
- Wooden spoon

Prize-Winning Chili-Mac Soup

Prep Time: 10 Minutes
Cook: 25 Minutes • 6 servings

Utensils

- Sharp knife
- 4-quart saucepan
- Dry-ingredient measuring cups
- Wooden spoon
- Colander
- Small bowl
- Liquid-ingredient measuring cup
- Measuring spoons
- Can opener

1 medium onion
¼ medium green bell pepper
1 pound lean (at least 80%) ground beef
5 cups hot water
1 box chili macaroni skillet-meal mix of pasta and tomato sauce mix with taco seasoning for hamburger
1 teaspoon chili powder
½ teaspoon garlic salt
2 cups diced tomatoes (from 28-ounce can)
1 can (11 ounces) vacuum-packed whole kernel corn with red and green peppers, undrained
2 tablespoons sliced pitted ripe olives

1 Place onion on cutting board. Using sharp knife, chop into small pieces to measure ½ cup. Chop bell pepper to measure ¼ cup. In 4-quart saucepan, cook ground beef, onion and bell pepper over medium-high heat 5 to 7 minutes, stirring occasionally with wooden spoon, until beef is brown and thoroughly cooked. Drain beef mixture in colander over a small bowl.

2 Stir in hot water, sauce mix (from box), chili powder, garlic salt and tomatoes.

   Heat to boiling, stirring occasionally.

3 Reduce heat to low; cover and simmer 5 minutes, stirring occasionally. Stir in the uncooked pasta (from box), corn and olives. Cover and cook 10 minutes longer or until pasta is tender.

Spoon this soup over some corn chips and shredded taco cheese, or sprinkle each serving of soup with corn chips or coarsely crushed tortilla chips.

1 Serving: Calories 330; Total Fat 10g (Saturated Fat 3.5g; Trans Fat 0.5g); Cholesterol 45mg; Sodium 990mg; Total Carbohydrate 40g (Dietary Fiber 3g); Protein 18g **Exchanges:** 2½ Starch, 1½ Medium-Fat Meat, ½ Fat **Carbohydrate Choices:** 2½

Movie-Time Cauliflower "Popcorn"

Prep Time: 10 Minutes • **Bake: 22 Minutes** • **3 servings (½ cup each)**

3   cups small fresh cauliflower florets

1   tablespoon olive or vegetable oil

¼   teaspoon salt

⅛   teaspoon black pepper

⅓   cup finely shredded sharp Cheddar cheese

1 Heat oven to 450°F. In large mixing bowl, combine cauliflower, oil, salt and pepper; stir with a wooden spoon until well mixed. Pour mixture evenly into ungreased 15×10×1-inch pan.

2 Bake 10 minutes. Use pot holders to take pan from oven. Using wooden spoon, stir cauliflower mixture. Return pan to oven. Bake 8 to 12 minutes longer until light golden brown and crisp-tender (use a fork to test). Sprinkle with cheese. Let stand about 1 minute or until cheese is melted.

1 Serving: Calories 120; Total Fat 9g (Saturated Fat 3.5g; Trans Fat 0g); Cholesterol 15mg; Sodium 310mg; Total Carbohydrate 6g (Dietary Fiber 2g); Protein 5g **Exchanges:** 1 Vegetable, ½ High-Fat Meat, 1 Fat **Carbohydrate Choices:** ½

If you like things a little spicier, try adding ⅛ teaspoon ground red pepper (cayenne).

Utensils

- Large mixing bowl
- Dry-ingredient measuring cups
- Measuring spoons
- Wooden spoon
- 15×10×1-inch pan
- Pot holders
- Cooling rack

Snacks

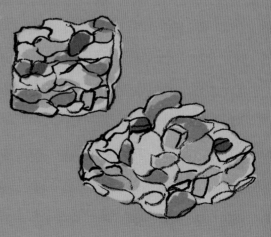

Party-Perfect Guacamole

Prep Time: 20 Minutes • **12 servings (¼ cup each)**

2   large ripe avocados
2   medium tomatoes
2   medium jalapeño chiles
1   medium onion
1   clove garlic
2   tablespoons finely chopped fresh cilantro
2   tablespoons lime or lemon juice
½   teaspoon salt
    Dash pepper
    Crispy horn-shaped corn snacks or tortilla chips, if you like

Utensils

- Cutting board
- Sharp knife
- Spoon
- Medium mixing bowl
- Fork
- Measuring spoons

1 Place avocados on cutting board. Cut each avocado in half lengthwise with sharp knife, cutting around the pit in center; using both hands, twist halves to separate the avocado. Scoop out pit using small spoon. Using spoon, scoop avocado from skin and place in medium mixing bowl. Mash avocado with fork until smooth but still just slightly chunky. Add all the remaining ingredients except corn snacks or chips; mix well.

2 Place tomatoes on cutting board. With sharp knife, chop into small pieces to measure 1½ cups. Using small spoon and paper towel, remove seeds from the jalapeño chiles and chop them finely. Be careful not to use your fingers to touch the chiles. Chop the onion to measure ½ cup and finely chop the garlic. Add tomatoes, chiles, onion, garlic, cilantro, lime juice, salt and pepper to avocado in bowl. Mix well.

3 Serve guacamole with corn snacks or chips.

1 Serving: Calories 50; Total Fat 3.5g (Saturated Fat 0g; Trans Fat 0g); Cholesterol 0mg; Sodium 100mg; Total Carbohydrate 4g (Dietary Fiber 2g); Protein 0g **Exchanges:** 1 Fat **Carbohydrate Choices:** 0

Honey Bear Dip

Prep Time: 5 Minutes • **Refrigerate: 1 Hour** • **12 servings (¼ cup each)**

3   cups vanilla yogurt
1   cup chopped unblanched whole almonds
1   tablespoon honey
½   teaspoon almond extract
     Fresh fruit, if you like

Utensils

- Wooden spoon
- Dry-ingredient measuring cups
- Measuring spoons
- Medium mixing bowl
- Plastic wrap

1 Using wooden spoon, mix all ingredients except fruit in medium mixing bowl. Cover with plastic wrap and refrigerate at least 1 hour but no longer than 24 hours.

2 Serve dip with fresh fruit.

1 Serving: Calories 130; Total Fat 6g (Saturated Fat 1g; Trans Fat 0g); Cholesterol 5mg; Sodium 35mg; Total Carbohydrate 15g (Dietary Fiber 1g); Protein 5g **Exchanges:** ½ Fruit, ½ Milk, 1 Fat **Carbohydrate Choices:** 1

Good choices of fruit include seedless grapes, whole strawberries and kiwifruit chunks. Banana chunks and pear and apple wedges (sprinkled with lemon juice to keep them from browning) are also yummy.

After-School Yogurt Hummus with Veggies

Prep Time: 15 Minutes • 6 servings (¼ cup each)

1 cup fresh sugar snap peas (¼ pound)

1 container (10 ounces) plain hummus

¼ cup plain Greek yogurt

¼ cup chopped red bell pepper

2 tablespoons chopped fresh parsley

½ teaspoon grated lemon peel

½ teaspoon lemon juice

⅛ teaspoon ground cumin

1 cup ready-to-eat baby-cut carrots

1 small yellow summer squash, sliced (about 1 cup)

Utensils

- 1-quart saucepan
- Colander
- Cutting board
- Sharp knife
- Scissors
- Grater
- Dry-ingredient measuring cups
- Medium mixing bowl
- Measuring spoons
- Wooden spoon
- Serving bowl

1. Fill 1-quart saucepan half full of water. Heat over high heat to boiling. Add peas; cook 1 minute. Drain peas in colander. Rinse with cold water; drain.

2. Place bell pepper on cutting board. Using sharp knife chop into small pieces to measure ¼ cup. Chop the parsley or use scissors to cut it up to measure 2 tablespoons. Use a grater to grate the lemon peel from the lemon to measure ½ teaspoon. Cut the lemon in half; squeeze one half into small bowl. Use ½ teaspoon.

3. In medium mixing bowl, combine hummus, yogurt, bell pepper, parsley, lemon peel, lemon juice and cumin; stir with wooden spoon until well mixed. Spoon into serving bowl. Sprinkle with more chopped parsley, if you like.

4. Serve with sugar snap peas, carrots and squash.

1 Serving: Calories 110; Total Fat 4.5g (Saturated Fat 0.5g; Trans Fat 0g); Cholesterol 0mg; Sodium 220mg; Total Carbohydrate 13g (Dietary Fiber 4g); Protein 5g **Exchanges:** ½ Other Carbohydrate, 1 Vegetable, ½ Very Lean Meat, 1 Fat **Carbohydrate Choices:** 1

Super Hero Smoothies

Prep Time: 5 Minutes • 2 servings

1½ cups vanilla soymilk

1 bag (10 ounces)
frozen strawberries,
partially thawed

1 medium banana

⅓ cup calcium-enriched
orange juice

Honey, if you like

Fresh strawberries,
if you like

Utensils

- Cutting board
- Table knife
- Blender or food processor
- Liquid-ingredient measuring cups
- 2 glasses
- 2 straws

1 Peel banana; place on cutting board. Use table knife to cut it into chunks. In blender or food processor, place soymilk, strawberries, banana and orange juice. Cover and blend on high speed about 1 minute or until smooth. Sweeten to taste with honey.

2 Pour into 2 glasses; garnish each with a fresh strawberry. Serve immediately.

1 Serving: Calories 210; Total Fat 3g (Saturated Fat 0g; Trans Fat 0g); Cholesterol 0mg; Sodium 90mg; Total Carbohydrate 40g (Dietary Fiber 5g); Protein 6g **Exchanges:** ½ Starch, 1 Fruit, 1 Other Carbohydrate, ½ Skim Milk, ½ Fat **Carbohydrate Choices:** 2½

Blueberry-Grape Smoothie Poppers

Prep Time: 15 Minutes • Refrigerate: 4 Hours • 24 servings

Cooking spray

2 envelopes unflavored gelatin

½ cup cold Concord grape juice

½ cup fresh blueberries

2 containers (6 ounces each) French vanilla low-fat yogurt

¾ cup Concord grape juice, heated to boiling

1 Lightly spray 9×5-inch loaf pan with cooking spray, then blot with a paper towel; set aside.

2 Place ½ cup cold grape juice in large mixing bowl; sprinkle gelatin over grape juice to soften; let stand 1 minute.

3 Meanwhile, in blender, place blueberries and yogurt. Cover; blend on high speed until smooth. Add ¾ cup hot grape juice to gelatin mixture and stir with wooden spoon about 2 minutes or until gelatin is dissolved. Stir in the yogurt mixture. Pour mixture into the loaf pan.

4 Cover with plastic wrap and refrigerate until firm, about 4 hours.

Cut into cubes with sharp knife and serve, or cover and refrigerate up to 2 days before serving.

Utensils

- 9×5-inch loaf pan
- Paper towel
- Liquid-ingredient measuring cup
- Large mixing bowl
- Blender
- Dry-ingredient measuring cups
- Wooden spoon
- Plastic wrap
- Small sharp knife

Blueberries are not only delicious and pretty, they are also a good source of fiber and vitamin C.

If you prefer Greek yogurt, use two containers (5.3 ounces each) vanilla Greek yogurt in place of the low-fat yogurt.

1 Serving: Calories 25; Total Fat 0g (Saturated Fat 0g; Trans Fat 0g); Cholesterol 0mg; Sodium 10mg; Total Carbohydrate 5g (Dietary Fiber 0g); Protein 1g **Exchanges:** ½ Starch **Carbohydrate Choices:** ½

Hiker's-Treat Trail Mix

Prep Time: 5 Minutes ● **8 servings (½ cup each)**

1 cup roasted soy nuts

1 cup oven-toasted wheat cereal squares

1 cup toasted multigrain or honey nut oat cereal

1 cup raisins or dried cranberries

½ cup candy-coated chocolate candies or chocolate chips

1 In large mixing bowl, combine all ingredients. Stir with wooden spoon to mix well.

2 Store in resealable food-storage bag or tightly covered container.

1 Serving: Calories 230; Total Fat 6g (Saturated Fat 2g; Trans Fat 0g); Cholesterol 0mg; Sodium 110mg; Total Carbohydrate 37g (Dietary Fiber 4g); Protein 6g **Exchanges:** 1½ Starch, 1 Other Carbohydrate, 1 Fat **Carbohydrate Choices:** 2½

Utensils

- Large mixing bowl
- Dry-ingredient measuring cups
- Wooden spoon
- Resealable food-storage bag

You can find crunchy roasted soy nuts in the bulk-foods section at your local supermarket or food cooperative.

Take-Along Oatmeal Bars

Prep Time: 15 Minutes
Cool: 30 Minutes • 16 bars

Butter for greasing
- ⅓ cup honey
- ¼ cup sugar
- ¼ cup butter
- ½ teaspoon ground cinnamon
- 1 cup diced dried fruit and raisin mixture
- 2 cups toasted whole wheat flake cereal
- 1 cup old-fashioned or quick-cooking oats
- ½ cup sliced almonds

Utensils

- Pastry brush
- 9-inch square pan
- 3-quart saucepan
- Liquid-ingredient measuring cup
- Dry-ingredient measuring cups
- Measuring spoons
- Wooden spoon
- Sharp knife

1 Use pastry brush or paper towel to grease bottom and sides of 9-inch square pan with small amount of butter.

2 In 3-quart saucepan, heat honey, sugar, butter and cinnamon to boiling over medium heat, stirring constantly with a wooden spoon. Boil 1 minute, stirring constantly. Remove from heat. Stir in dried fruit. Stir in remaining ingredients.

3 Press mixture in pan with back of wooden spoon. Cool completely, about 30 minutes. For bars, cut into 4 rows by 4 rows. Store loosely covered at room temperature.

1 Bar: Calories 140; Total Fat 5g (Saturated Fat 2g; Trans Fat 0g); Cholesterol 10mg; Sodium 55mg; Total Carbohydrate 22g (Dietary Fiber 2g); Protein 2g **Exchanges:** ½ Starch, 1 Other Carbohydrate, 1 Fat **Carbohydrate Choices:** 1½

These yummy bars contain both ready-to-eat cereal and oats, two great whole grains that are terrific together. Pack a couple bars in your backpack or lunch box for an any-time-of-day snack.

Energy-Boost Granola Fruit Kabobs

Prep Time: 10 Minutes • 8 servings

2 cups granola
1 cup fruit-flavored yogurt
2 medium apples, unpeeled
2 small bananas, peeled
1 cup fresh pineapple chunks

Utensils

- Cutting board
- Sharp knife
- Dry-ingredient measuring cups
- 2 shallow bowls
- Toothpicks

1 Place granola in shallow bowl. Place yogurt in a separate shallow bowl.

2 Place apples on cutting board. Using sharp knife, cut into chunks. Cut bananas into chunks. Insert a toothpick into each piece of fruit. Dip each fruit piece into yogurt, coating all sides. Roll each in granola, coating completely.

To prevent cut fruits such as bananas and apples from browning, toss the pieces with a small amount of lemon or orange juice.

1 Serving: Calories 200; Total Fat 5g (Saturated Fat 2g; Trans Fat 0g); Cholesterol 0mg; Sodium 30mg; Total Carbohydrate 35g (Dietary Fiber 4g); Protein 4g **Exchanges:** 1 Starch, ½ Fruit, 1 Other Carbohydrate, 1 Fat **Carbohydrate Choices:** 2

Corny Bacon and Cheese Pinwheel Snacks

Prep Time: 15 Minutes • Bake: 17 Minutes • 12 pinwheels

Cooking spray

1 can (8 ounces) refrigerated crescent dinner rolls

1 package (3 ounces) cream cheese, softened

⅔ cup shredded Cheddar cheese

½ cup frozen corn, thawed, drained

4 slices cooked bacon

1 Heat oven to 350°F. Spray cookie sheet with cooking spray.

2 Follow directions on can to open and remove dough. Unroll dough onto cookie sheet. Firmly press the perforations with your fingers to seal. Using table knife, spread cream cheese over dough rectangle; sprinkle with Cheddar cheese and corn. With fingers, crumble bacon. Sprinkle over top.

3 Starting with long side, roll up rectangle; press edge with fingers to seal.

With serrated knife, cut roll into 12 slices, each about 1-inch thick; place cut side down on cookie sheet.

4 Bake 13 to 17 minutes or until edges are golden brown.

1 Pinwheel: Calories 130; Total Fat 8g (Saturated Fat 4.5g; Trans Fat 0g); Cholesterol 15mg; Sodium 260mg; Total Carbohydrate 10g (Dietary Fiber 0g); Protein 4g **Exchanges:** ½ Other Carbohydrate, ½ High-Fat Meat, 1 Fat **Carbohydrate Choices:** ½

Utensils

- Cookie sheet
- Table knife
- Dry-ingredient measuring cups
- Serrated knife
- Ruler
- Hot pads
- Cooling rack

These cheesy, corny pinwheels are a great snack on their own or a perfect side to your favorite soup or chili.

Hoppin' Poppin' Popcorn

Whether you're planning to watch a movie, just coming in from outdoor activities or need an after-school snack, popcorn fits the bill. We love it plain or with a little salt and butter, but why not pop up some and top it in a new way?

To make 12 to 16 cups of popped corn, place ½ cup unpopped kernels in a 4-quart saucepan and add 3 to 4 tablespoons vegetable oil. Toss the kernels until they are coated with the oil. Cover the pan and cook over medium-high heat until the kernels start to pop. Start carefully shaking the pan to move the popcorn around as it pops. Cook and shake until the popcorn stops popping. Pour into a big bowl and add whatever you like—here are some yummy ideas (besides salt and butter).

Just Sprinkle and Toss

Shredded Parmesan or Cheddar cheese (about ¼ cup)

Chili powder (½ to 1 teaspoon)

Italian seasoning (1 to 2 teaspoons)

Cinnamon-sugar (1 to 2 teaspoons)

Toss to Mix

Favorite oat, rice or multi-grain cereal (1 to 2 cups)

Fruit-flavored corn puff cereal (1 to 2 cups)

Granola (1 to 2 cups)

Raisins or dried cranberries (½ to 1 cup)

Peanuts (plain or honey-roasted) or cashews (½ to 1 cup)

Mini pretzels (1 to 1½ cups)

Shelled sunflower seeds or roasted soy nuts (½ cup)

Candy-coated chocolate pieces (½ to 1 cup)

Garden-Fun Kale Chips

Prep Time: 15 Minutes • Bake: 15 Minutes • 6 servings

1   **bunch (about ½ pound) fresh kale**

¼   **cup grated Parmesan cheese**

⅛   **teaspoon crushed red pepper flakes**

⅛   **teaspoon dried oregano leaves**

⅛   **teaspoon salt**
     Cooking spray

Utensils

- Paper towels
- Cutting board
- Small sharp knife
- Dry-measuring cups
- Large mixing bowl
- Small mixing bowl
- Measuring spoons
- Wooden spoon
- 2 cookie sheets
- Pot holders
- Cooling rack

1 Heat oven to 350°F. Wash kale leaves under cool running water; pat dry with paper towels.

On cutting board, using small sharp knife, cut rib (the thick center part of each leaf) from each kale leaf. Tear leaves into 1- to 2-inch pieces to equal 6 cups; place in a large mixing bowl.

2 In small mixing bowl, mix Parmesan cheese, pepper flakes, oregano and salt. Spray the kale leaves with short bursts of cooking spray, tossing and spraying until lightly coated. Sprinkle with cheese mixture; toss to combine with wooden spoon.

3 Place kale in single layer on ungreased cookie sheet. (You may need to use 2 cookie sheets.)

Bake 1 cookie sheet at a time 12 to 15 minutes or until crisp. Cool 5 minutes before serving.

1 Serving: Calories 60; Total Fat 1.5g (Saturated Fat 1g; Trans Fat 0g); Cholesterol 0mg; Sodium 150mg; Total Carbohydrate 7g (Dietary Fiber 1g); Protein 4g **Exchanges:** ½ Other Carbohydrate, ½ Vegetable, ½ Lean Meat **Carbohydrate Choices:** ½

Store the kale chips at room temperature in a paper bag to retain crispness longer. If chips lose their crunch, heat in a 325°F oven for 3 to 5 minutes on a cookie sheet.

Fruity Frozen Bananas

Prep Time: 10 Minutes • Freeze: 1 Hour • 8 servings

4 firm ripe bananas

1 to 2 containers (6 ounces each) thick and creamy yogurt (any flavor)

3 cups toasted whole grain fruity cereal

Utensils

- Cookie sheet
- Waxed paper
- Cutting board
- Table knife
- 8 flat wooden sticks with round ends
- 2 shallow bowls
- Dry-ingredient measuring cup
- Plastic wrap or foil

1. Cover cookie sheet with waxed paper. Peel bananas; place on cutting board. Cut each banana crosswise in half with a table knife. Insert a wooden stick into the cut end of each banana.

2. Place yogurt in a shallow bowl. Place cereal in a separate shallow bowl. Roll bananas in the yogurt, then in the cereal to coat. Place bananas on cookie sheet. Freeze until firm, about 1 hour.

3. Wrap each banana in plastic wrap or foil. Store in freezer.

1 Serving: Calories 120; Total Fat 1g (Saturated Fat 0g; Trans Fat 0g); Cholesterol 0mg; Sodium 90mg; Total Carbohydrate 26g (Dietary Fiber 3g); Protein 3g **Exchanges:** ½ Starch, 1 Other Carbohydrate **Carbohydrate Choices:** 2

Try different flavors of yogurt like strawberry, peach, vanilla or another favorite flavor.

Dinner

Mighty Mini Meat Loaves

Prep Time: 10 Minutes ● **Bake: 20 Minutes** ● **6 servings (2 loaves each)**

- ½ cup ketchup
- 2 tablespoons packed brown sugar
- 1 pound lean (at least 80%) ground beef
- ½ pound ground pork
- ½ cup all-purpose baking mix
- ¼ teaspoon pepper
- 1 small onion, finely chopped (⅓ cup)
- 1 egg
  Cooking spray

1 Heat oven to 450°F. In small mixing bowl, combine the ketchup and brown sugar; stir with rubber spatula until mixed. Set aside ¼ cup for topping. In large mixing bowl, stir remaining ketchup mixture with all of the remaining ingredients with wooden spoon until well mixed.

2 Spray 13×9-inch pan with cooking spray. Place meat mixture in pan; pat into 12×4-inch rectangle using your hands. Cut mixture in half the long way using a table knife. Cut into 6 rows the short way. You should have 12 small loaves. Separate loaves a little, using table knife, so no edges are touching. Brush loaves with the ¼ cup ketchup mixture that was set aside.

3 👆 Bake 18 to 20 minutes or until loaves are no longer pink in center and a meat thermometer placed in the center of each loaf reads 160°F. Use pot holders to remove pan from oven.

1 Serving: Calories 300; Total Fat 16g (Saturated Fat 6g; Trans Fat 1g); Cholesterol 105mg; Sodium 430mg; Total Carbohydrate 16g (Dietary Fiber 0g); Protein 22g **Exchanges:** ½ Starch, ½ Other Carbohydrate, 3 Medium-Fat Meat **Carbohydrate Choices:** 1

These little loaves bake much faster than a traditional whole meat loaf, plus you get more of that tangy crust. Stick with the "mini" theme by serving small boiled potatoes and cooked baby-cut carrots (both of which also cook up extra-fast!).

Utensils

- Small mixing bowl
- Rubber spatula
- Dry-ingredient measuring cups
- Measuring spoons
- Large mixing bowl
- Wooden spoon
- Ruler
- Table knife
- Pastry brush
- Pot holders
- Meat thermometer

Impossibly Easy Mini Chicken Pot Pies

Prep Time: 20 Minutes • **Bake: 30 Minutes**
Cool: 15 Minutes • **6 servings (2 mini pies each)**

Cooking spray
1 tablespoon vegetable oil
1 pound boneless skinless chicken breasts, cut into bite-size pieces
1 medium onion, chopped (½ cup)
½ cup chicken broth
1 cup frozen peas and carrots
½ teaspoon salt
¼ teaspoon pepper
¼ teaspoon ground thyme
1 cup shredded Cheddar cheese
½ cup all-purpose baking mix
½ cup milk
2 eggs

Utensils

- 12-cup muffin pan
- 10-inch nonstick skillet
- Measuring spoons
- Wooden spoon
- Liquid-ingredient measuring cup
- Dry-ingredient measuring cups
- Medium mixing bowl
- Whisk or fork
- Spoon
- Toothpick
- Thin knife
- Pot holders
- Cooling rack

1. Heat oven to 375°F. Spray 12 regular-size muffin cups with cooking spray.

2. 🧤 In 10-inch nonstick skillet, heat oil over medium-high heat. Cook chicken in oil 5 to 7 minutes, stirring occasionally with wooden spoon, until chicken is no longer pink in center. Add onion and chicken broth; heat to simmering. Add frozen vegetables and seasonings. Heat until hot, stirring occasionally until almost all liquid is absorbed. Cool 5 minutes; stir in cheese.

3. In medium mixing bowl, stir baking mix, milk and eggs with whisk or fork until blended. Spoon slightly less than 1 tablespoon of the dough into each muffin cup. Top with about ¼ cup of the chicken mixture. Spoon 1 tablespoon dough onto chicken mixture in each muffin cup.

4. Bake 25 to 30 minutes or until toothpick inserted in center comes out clean. Cool in pan 5 minutes. With thin knife, loosen sides of pies from pan; remove from pan and place top side up on cooling rack. Cool 10 minutes longer but serve warm.

1 Serving: Calories 290; Total Fat 15g (Saturated Fat 6g; Trans Fat 0.5g); Cholesterol 130mg; Sodium 600mg; Total Carbohydrate 12g (Dietary Fiber 1g); Protein 26g **Exchanges:** ½ Starch, ½ Vegetable, 3 Very Lean Meat, ½ High-Fat Meat, 2 Fat **Carbohydrate Choices:** 1

Kickin' Chicken Tenders with Gorgonzola Dip

Prep Time: 10 Minutes • **Bake: 15 Minutes**

16 servings (1 tender and 1 heaping tablespoon dip each)

1	cup sour cream
2	tablespoons lemon juice
1	teaspoon ground red pepper (cayenne)
1⅓	cups Italian-style crispy bread crumbs
1	package (14 ounces) chicken tenders
½	cup mayonnaise or salad dressing
½	cup crumbled gorgonzola cheese (2 ounces)
2	tablespoons chopped fresh parsley
1	tablespoon milk

1 Heat oven to 400°F. Spray large cookie sheet with cooking spray. In small shallow bowl, stir together ½ cup of the sour cream, 1 tablespoon of the lemon juice and ½ teaspoon of the red pepper until blended. In 1-gallon resealable food-storage plastic bag, combine bread crumbs and ¼ teaspoon of the red pepper.

2 On cutting board cut each chicken tender in half crosswise. Dip each chicken piece in sour-cream mixture. Place 4 chicken pieces at a time in bag with bread crumbs. Seal bag; shake to coat. Place coated chicken pieces on cookie sheet. Repeat with remaining chicken, sour-cream mixture and bread crumbs.

Bake 12 to 15 minutes or until chicken is no longer pink in center and coating is golden brown.

3 While the chicken is cooking, in small mixing bowl, stir together the remaining ½ cup sour cream, 1 tablespoon lemon juice, remaining ¼ teaspoon red pepper, the mayonnaise, cheese and parsley until blended; stir in milk. Serve dip with tenders.

1 Serving: Calories 150; Total Fat 10g (Saturated Fat 3.5g; Trans Fat 0g); Cholesterol 25mg; Sodium 290mg; Total Carbohydrate 8g (Dietary Fiber 0g); Protein 8g **Exchanges:** ½ Starch, 1 Very Lean Meat, 2 Fat **Carbohydrate Choices:** ½

Utensils

- Large cookie sheet
- Small shallow bowl
- Dry-ingredient measuring cups
- Measuring spoons
- 1-gallon resealable food-storage plastic bag
- Small mixing bowl
- Cutting board
- Small sharp knife
- Pot holders
- Cooling rack

You can make this recipe ahead if you like. Make the dip as directed, then cover and refrigerate up to 1 day. Make the chicken tenders just to the point of baking. Cover and refrigerate up to 4 hours. Uncover and bake them right before serving.

Salmon Nuggets with Creamy Dill Dip

Prep Time: 20 Minutes   **Bake: 15 Minutes**   **12 servings (3 nuggets and 1 tablespoon dip each)**

Salmon

- ½ cup all-purpose flour
- ½ teaspoon salt
- ⅛ teaspoon ground black pepper
- 1 cup unseasoned panko bread crumbs
- ½ cup shredded Parmesan cheese
- 1 tablespoon chopped fresh parsley
- 2 eggs
- 1 pound salmon fillets, skin removed

Dip

- ½ cup sour cream
- ¼ cup mayonnaise or salad dressing
- 1½ tablespoons chopped fresh dill weed

1 Heat oven to 450°F. Line large cookie sheet with cooking parchment paper.

2 In shallow bowl or dish, place the flour, salt and pepper; stir with wooden spoon until mixed. In small mixing bowl, place the panko crumbs, Parmesan cheese and parsley; stir with wooden spoon until mixed.

3 Place eggs in another shallow bowl; beat well with whisk or fork.

Place salmon on cutting board. Using sharp knife, cut salmon into 1-inch cubes. Coat salmon pieces in flour mixture; shake off excess. Using 2 forks dip in eggs and then in crumb mixture, gently pressing into salmon. Place on cookie sheet.

4 Bake 12 to 15 minutes or until golden brown. Use pot holders to remove pan from oven.

5 Meanwhile, in small mixing bowl, combine dip ingredients, and stir until well blended. Serve with salmon nuggets.

1 Serving: Calories 200; Total Fat 11g (Saturated Fat 3.5g; Trans Fat 0g); Cholesterol 60mg; Sodium 250mg; Total Carbohydrate 11g (Dietary Fiber 0g); Protein 12g **Exchanges:** ½ Starch, ½ Lean Meat, 1 Medium-Fat Meat, 1 Fat **Carbohydrate Choices:** 1

Honey Mustard Dip Omit the dill weed and add 2 tablespoons honey mustard for a sweeter and spicier dip.

Utensils

- Large cookie sheet
- Cooking parchment paper
- Cutting board
- Sharp knife
- Shallow bowl or dish
- Dry-ingredient measuring cups
- Measuring spoons
- Wooden spoon
- 2 small mixing bowls
- Whisk or fork
- Shallow bowl
- Pot holders
- Cooling rack

Utensils

- 10-inch skillet
- Liquid-ingredient measuring cup
- Measuring spoons
- Dry-ingredient measuring cup
- Can opener
- Colander
- Spoon

Say Cheese! Salsa-Rice Burritos

Prep Time: 15 Minutes • **Stand: 5 Minutes** • **8 burritos**

1½ cups chunky-style salsa

1½ teaspoons chili powder

1 cup uncooked instant rice

1 can (15 ounces) black beans

1 can (11 ounces) whole kernel corn with red and green peppers, undrained

1½ cups shredded Cheddar cheese (6 ounces)

8 flour tortillas (8 inch)

Additional salsa, if you like

1 In 10-inch skillet, heat 1½ cups salsa and the chili powder to boiling. Stir in rice; remove from heat. Cover; let stand 5 minutes.

2 With can opener, open cans of beans and corn. Pour beans into colander to drain. Rinse with cold water. Stir beans, corn and cheese into rice mixture.

3 Place tortillas on clean counter. Spoon about ½ cup rice mixture on center of each tortilla. Roll tortillas around filling; tuck ends under. Serve with additional salsa.

1 Burrito: Calories 390; Total Fat 11g (Saturated Fat 5g; Trans Fat 0.5g); Cholesterol 20mg; Sodium 680mg; Total Carbohydrate 58g (Dietary Fiber 6g); Protein 16g **Exchanges:** 4 Starch, ½ Very Lean Meat, 1½ Fat **Carbohydrate Choices:** 4

Wild-Ride Chicken Nugget Tacos

Prep Time: 30 Minutes • **6 servings**
(2 tacos each)

- 24 frozen breaded cooked chicken nuggets
- ¼ cup sour cream
- 2 teaspoons 40%-less-sodium taco seasoning mix (from 1-ounce package)
- 1 to 2 tablespoons milk
- 1 box (7.4 ounces) hard and soft taco shells (6 hard corn shells and 6 soft flour tortillas)
- ¾ cup shredded Cheddar cheese
- 1½ cups shredded lettuce
- ½ cup chunky-style salsa

Utensils

- Cookie sheet
- Pot holders
- Foil
- Small mixing bowl
- Dry-ingredient measuring cups
- Measuring spoons
- Wooden spoon
- Spoon

1 Bake chicken nuggets as directed on package. Cover with foil to keep warm. Reduce oven temperature to 325°F. Heat taco shells and tortillas as directed on box.

2 Meanwhile, in small mixing bowl, combine sour cream and taco seasoning mix. Add enough milk to make desired consistency and stir with wooden spoon to mix well. Set aside.

3 Fill each taco shell and tortilla with 2 chicken nuggets, cheese, lettuce and salsa. Drizzle each with sour cream mixture.

1 Serving: Calories 400; Total Fat 24g (Saturated Fat 7g; Trans Fat 1g); Cholesterol 45mg; Sodium 890mg; Total Carbohydrate 31g (Dietary Fiber 1g); Protein 16g **Exchanges:** 2 Starch, 1½ Lean Meat, 3½ Fat **Carbohydrate Choices:** 2

If you like, spice up these tacos a bit more by using shredded Mexican cheese blend and hot salsa.

Camp-In Pizza Burgers

Prep Time: 20 Minutes   6 sandwiches

1   medium onion
1   small green bell pepper
1   pound lean (at least 80%) ground beef
1   jar (14 ounces) or can (15 ounces) pepperoni-flavored or regular pizza sauce
½   cup sliced ripe olives, if you like
6   burger buns, split
¾   cup shredded pizza cheese blend

1 Place onion on cutting board. Using sharp knife, chop into small pieces to measure ½ cup. Chop bell pepper to measure ½ cup. In 10-inch skillet, cook beef, onion and bell pepper over medium heat 8 to 10 minutes, stirring occasionally with wooden spoon, until beef is thoroughly cooked; drain beef in colander over a small bowl.

2 Return cooked ground beef to skillet. Stir in pizza sauce and olives. Heat to boiling, stirring occasionally.

3 Spoon beef mixture on bottom half of each bun. Immediately sprinkle each with 2 tablespoons cheese; cover with top halves of buns. Serve immediately, or let stand about 2 minutes until cheese is melted.

1 Sandwich: Calories 350; Total Fat 16g (Saturated Fat 6g; Trans Fat 1g); Cholesterol 60mg; Sodium 670mg; Total Carbohydrate 29g (Dietary Fiber 2g); Protein 22g **Exchanges:** 2 Starch, 2½ Medium-Fat Meat, ½ Fat **Carbohydrate Choices:** 2

Utensils

- Cutting board
- Sharp knife
- 10-inch skillet
- Wooden spoon
- Colander
- Small bowl
- Dry-ingredient measuring cups
- Measuring spoons

Turkey Cheeseburger Sliders

Prep Time: 10 Minutes • Cook: 10 Minutes • 6 servings (2 sliders each)

1 pound ground turkey

1 cup unseasoned dry bread crumbs

1 teaspoon Montreal steak seasoning (or other all-purpose seasoning)

1 pouch (9 ounces) creamy three-cheese cooking sauce

Sliced cheese, your favorite kind (American, pepper Jack, Cheddar), if you like

12 slider buns

Sliced tomato, sliced onion, leaf lettuce, pickles, ketchup and mustard, if you like

Utensils

- Large mixing bowl
- Dry-ingredient measuring cup
- Measuring spoons
- Wooden spoon
- 12-inch nonstick skillet
- Pancake turner
- Meat thermometer

1. In large mixing bowl, combine ground turkey, bread crumbs, seasoning and cooking sauce; stir using wooden spoon until well mixed. With hands, shape into 12 patties.

2. Heat 12-inch nonstick skillet over medium heat. Place patties in skillet. Cook 4 to 5 minutes on each side, turning once with pancake turner, or until browned and cooked through and meat thermometer placed in center of each patty reads 165°F. Top patties with cheese slices. Serve on slider buns with remaining ingredients.

1 Serving: Calories 400; Total Fat 14g (Saturated Fat 3.5g; Trans Fat 0g); Cholesterol 60mg; Sodium 730mg; Total Carbohydrate 45g (Dietary Fiber 2g); Protein 24g **Exchanges:** 3 Starch, ½ Very Lean Meat, 1½ Lean Meat, 1½ Fat **Carbohydrate Choices:** 3

The ground turkey mixture will be moist. You can assemble the patties ahead of time, and refrigerate 30 minutes to help them set up before cooking.

All 12 sliders will fit into 1 skillet, but feel free to cook in 2 separate batches if it's easier.

Cheese-Stuffed Meatballs and Spaghetti

Freeze: 1 Hour • **Prep Time: 35 Minutes**
Bake: 10 Minutes • **Cook: 10 Minutes** • **6 servings**

Cooking spray

4 sticks (1 ounce each) mozzarella string cheese, cut into 18 (¾-inch) cubes

½ cup Italian-style dry bread crumbs

1 jar (48 ounces) tomato pasta sauce (any flavor)

1½ pounds lean (at least 80%) ground beef

2 tablespoons finely chopped onion

½ teaspoon salt

½ teaspoon dried oregano leaves

1 egg

12 ounces uncooked spaghetti

⅔ cup shredded fresh Parmesan cheese

1 Place cheese cubes in small resealable freezer plastic bag; seal bag and freeze at least 1 hour.

2 Heat oven to 375°F. Line a 15×10×1-inch pan with foil; spray the foil with cooking spray. In large mixing bowl, mix bread crumbs and 3 tablespoons of the pasta sauce. Stir in ground beef, onion, salt, oregano and egg. Using hands, shape mixture into 18 (2-inch) balls. Press 1 cheese cube into center of each ball, sealing it inside. Gently place on foil in pan.

👈 Bake 10 minutes. Use pot holders to remove pan from oven.

3 Meanwhile, pour the remaining pasta sauce into 5-quart saucepot. Cover; simmer over medium-high heat, stirring frequently with wooden spoon. Gently stir in meatballs with

wooden spoon; reduce heat to medium-low. Cover; simmer about 10 minutes, stirring occasionally, until meatballs are thoroughly cooked and no longer pink.

4 Meanwhile, in 4-quart saucepan, cook and drain spaghetti as directed on package; keep warm.

5 Serve meatballs and sauce over spaghetti. Serve with Parmesan cheese.

1 Serving: Calories 850; Total Fat 30g (Saturated Fat 11g; Trans Fat 1g); Cholesterol 125mg; Sodium 2050mg; Total Carbohydrate 99g (Dietary Fiber 6g); Protein 44g **Exchanges:** 4½ Starch, 2 Other Carbohydrate, 4 Medium-Fat Meat, 1½ Fat **Carbohydrate Choices:** 6½

Utensils

- Sharp knife
- Small resealable freezer plastic bag
- 15×10×1-inch pan
- Foil
- Large mixing bowl
- Dry-ingredient measuring cups
- Measuring spoons
- Ruler
- Pot holders
- Cooling rack
- 5-quart saucepot
- 4-quart saucepan
- Wooden spoon

Snow-Day Chicken Chili

Prep Time: 15 Minutes • **Cook: 4 Hours 15 Minutes** • **8 servings**

- 6   bone-in chicken thighs (1½ pounds)
- 1   large onion, chopped (1 cup)
- 2   cloves garlic, finely chopped
-     Cooking spray
- 1¾ cups chicken broth (from 32-ounce carton)
- 1   teaspoon ground cumin
- 1   teaspoon dried oregano leaves
- ½   teaspoon salt
- ¼   teaspoon red pepper sauce
- 2   cans (15 to 16 ounces each) great northern beans, drained, rinsed
- 1   can (11 ounces) vacuum-packed white shoepeg corn, drained
- 3   tablespoons lime juice
- 2   tablespoons chopped fresh cilantro

Utensils

- Cutting board
- Sharp knife
- Paper towels
- 3½- to 4-quart slow cooker
- Liquid-ingredient measuring cup
- Measuring spoons
- Large bowl
- 2 forks
- Can opener
- Colander

1. Using a paper towel, grab the chicken skin and remove with excess fat from chicken. Use a small sharp knife to help cut away if necessary.

   Place onion on cutting board. Using sharp knife, chop to measure 1 cup. Finely chop garlic. Spray 3½- to 4-quart slow cooker with cooking spray. In slow cooker, mix onion, garlic, broth, cumin, oregano, salt and red pepper sauce. Top with chicken.

2. Cover; cook on Low heat setting 4 to 5 hours.

3. Remove chicken from slow cooker and place in large bowl. Use 2 forks to remove bones and shred chicken into pieces. Return shredded chicken to slow cooker; discard bones. Stir beans, corn and lime juice into mixture in slow cooker.

4. Cover; cook on Low heat setting 15 to 20 minutes longer or until beans and corn are hot. Sprinkle with cilantro.

1 Serving: Calories 270; Total Fat 5g (Saturated Fat 1.5g; Trans Fat 0g); Cholesterol 35mg; Sodium 470mg; Total Carbohydrate 33g (Dietary Fiber 7g); Protein 23g **Exchanges:** 2 Starch, 2½ Very Lean Meat, ½ Fat **Carbohydrate Choices:** 2

Soup's On!

You thought soup was hard to make? It's not, and you can even add your favorite foods to make it just as you like it. Use this simple formula, and before you know it, there will be warm soup just simmering with flavor and aroma.

Start with 4 cups of broth (vegetable, chicken or beef) in a soup pot. Heat it to a boil over medium heat. Then add ½ to 1 cup of veggies like:

Chopped carrots

Sliced celery

Chopped green or red bell pepper

Chunks of potato (peeled or unpeeled)

Chopped onion (just ¼ cup)

Sliced fresh mushrooms

Frozen cut green beans

Frozen peas or corn

Frozen small broccoli or cauliflower florets

Then add about 1 cup diced or cut-up cooked meat—these are good choices:

Chicken or turkey

Beef

Italian sausage

Ham or Canadian bacon

Simmer the soup uncovered (on low heat) until the veggies are tender when tested with a fork. Then you can add other things that you like:

Cooked beans or lentils (½ cup)

Uncooked small pasta like alphabet shapes or small macaroni (½ cup)

Cooked brown or white rice (½ cup)

Simmer 10 to 15 minutes longer until all is hot and everything is tender, stirring 2 or 3 times.

Sky-High Mac and Cheese with Broccoli

Prep Time: 10 Minutes • **3 servings (⅔ cup each)**

½ cup uncooked
   elbow macaroni

1 box (10 ounces) frozen
   broccoli and cheese sauce

Utensils

- 2-quart saucepan
- Colander
- Wooden spoon

1 In 2-quart saucepan, cook macaroni as directed on package. Drain well in colander. Return macaroni to saucepan.

2 While macaroni is cooking, cook broccoli as directed on box. Stir broccoli with cheese sauce into macaroni using wooden spoon.

1 Serving: Calories 140; Total Fat 2.5g (Saturated Fat 1g, Trans Fat 0g); Cholesterol 0mg; Sodium 360mg; Total Carbohydrate 24g (Dietary Fiber 2g); Protein 5g **Exchanges:** 1 Starch, ½ Other Carbohydrate, 1 Vegetable, ½ Fat **Carbohydrate Choices:** 1½

Utensils

- 4-quart saucepan
- Colander
- Large mixing bowl
- Can opener
- Dry-ingredient measuring cups
- Measuring spoons
- Wooden spoon
- Plastic wrap

Irresistible Tuna-Macaroni Salad

Prep Time: 20 Minutes • **Refrigerate: 1 Hour** • **6 servings (1 cup each)**

1 package (7 ounces) elbow macaroni

½ cup frozen green peas, thawed

1 can (9 ounces) tuna, drained

1 cup mayonnaise or salad dressing

1 cup shredded Cheddar cheese, if you like

¼ cup sweet pickle relish, if you like

2 teaspoons lemon juice

¾ teaspoon salt

¼ teaspoon pepper

1 medium stalk celery, chopped (½ cup)

1 small onion, chopped (⅓ cup)

1 In 4-quart saucepan, cook macaroni as directed on package, adding peas during the last 4 to 6 minutes of cooking. Drain macaroni and peas in colander and rinse with cold water; drain.

2 In large mixing bowl, mix macaroni, peas and all remaining ingredients; stir with wooden spoon until well mixed. Cover with plastic wrap and refrigerate at least 1 hour to blend flavors.

1 Serving: Calories 450; Total Fat 30g (Saturated Fat 4.5g; Trans Fat 0g); Cholesterol 35mg; Sodium 780mg; Total Carbohydrate 29g (Dietary Fiber 3g); Protein 15g **Exchanges:** 2 Starch, 1½ Very Lean Meat, 5½ Fat **Carbohydrate Choices:** 2

Fresh-from-the-Market Roasted Vegetables

Prep Time: 15 Minutes
Roast: 35 Minutes • 10 servings (½ cup each)

¼ cup olive or vegetable oil
¾ teaspoon lemon pepper
½ teaspoon sea salt or regular salt
½ teaspoon dried thyme leaves
2 cups small Brussels sprouts
1 bag (16-ounces) cubed sweet potatoes (about 3½ cups)
3 cups cauliflower florets

Utensils

- Large mixing bowl
- Liquid-ingredient measuring cup
- Measuring spoons
- Wooden spoon
- Cutting board
- Small sharp knife
- Dry-ingredient measuring cup
- 15×10×1-inch pan
- Pot holders
- Cooling rack

1 Heat oven to 425°F. In large mixing bowl, place oil, lemon pepper, salt and thyme. Stir with wooden spoon until mixed. Place Brussels sprouts on cutting board. With small sharp knife, cut each one in half. Add Brussels sprouts, sweet potatoes and cauliflower to oil mixture; stir until vegetables are well coated. Pour into ungreased 15×10×1-inch pan.

2 Roast uncovered 30 to 35 minutes, stirring once, until vegetables are tender and start to brown. Use pot holders to remove pan from oven.

1 Serving: Calories 110; Total Fat 6g (Saturated Fat 1g; Trans Fat 0g); Cholesterol 0mg; Sodium 180mg; Total Carbohydrate 12g (Dietary Fiber 2g); Protein 1g **Exchanges:** ½ Other Carbohydrate, 1 Vegetable, 1 Fat **Carbohydrate Choices:** 1

TODAY'S
SPECIALS
SWEET
POTATOES   89¢/lb
BRUSSEL
SPROUTS   99¢/lb

CAULIFLOWER   49¢/lb

123

Starburst Veggie Salad

Prep Time: 10 Minutes • **1 serving (1 salad)**

Dressing

⅓ cup buttermilk

¼ cup plain Greek yogurt

2 tablespoons mayonnaise or salad dressing

1 teaspoon fresh chopped parsley

⅛ teaspoon coarse ground pepper

⅛ teaspoon sea salt

Salad

1 cup mixed baby salad greens

¼ medium avocado

¼ medium red bell pepper

1 miniature Persian cucumber

1 yellow cherry tomato

Utensils

- Pint jar or bottle with lid
- Liquid-ingredient measuring cup
- Dry-ingredient measuring cups
- Measuring spoons
- Cutting board
- Small sharp knife
- Serving plate

1 In pint jar or bottle with lid, combine dressing ingredients until well mixed; cover with lid and shake well. Set aside.

2 Place salad greens on serving plate. Place avocado on cutting board. With small sharp knife, cut in half lengthwise; with hands, split to separate halves. Using small spoon scoop out pit and discard. Remove peel with fingers. Cut avocado into thin slices. Cut bell pepper into thin strips. Cut enough cucumber slices to measure ⅛ cup. Arrange avocado slices, bell pepper strips and cucumber slices in spoke fashion on the salad greens. Place the tomato in center of spoke. Drizzle with dressing. Store any remaining dressing in refrigerator.

1 Serving: Calories 380; Total Fat 30g (Saturated Fat 6g; Trans Fat 0g); Cholesterol 20mg; Sodium 580mg; Total Carbohydrate 15g (Dietary Fiber 4g); Protein 12g **Exchanges:** ½ Low-Fat Milk, 1½ Vegetable, ½ Very Lean Meat, 5½ Fat **Carbohydrate Choices:** 1

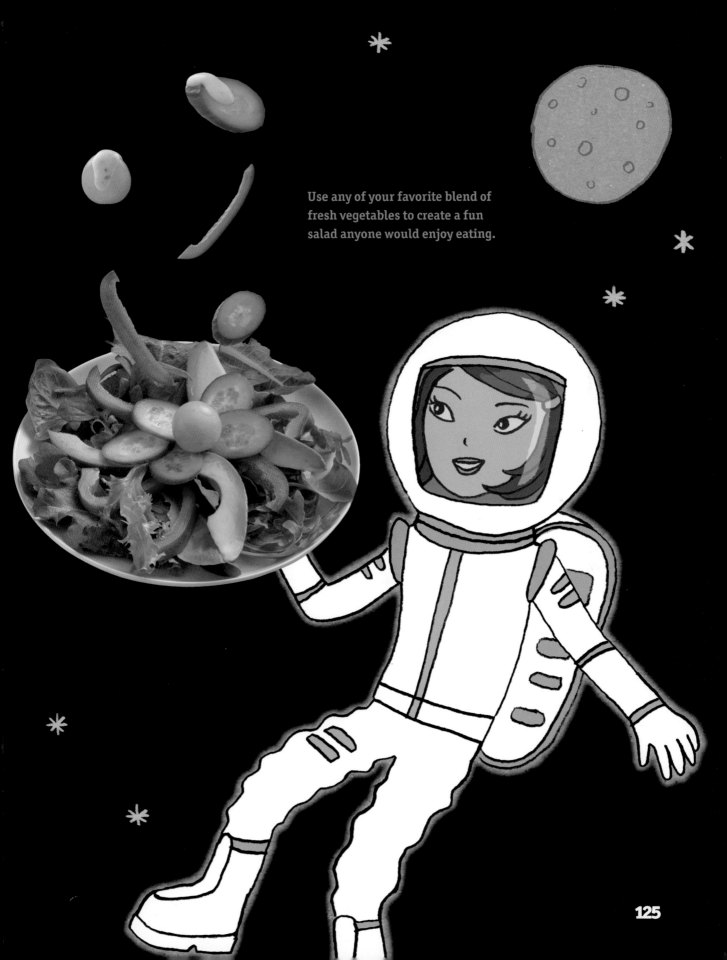

Use any of your favorite blend of fresh vegetables to create a fun salad anyone would enjoy eating.

Desserts

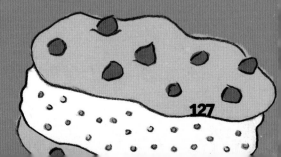

Traditional baking apples such as Granny Smith, Rome Beauty and Greening can also be used for a less-sweet treat.

Harvest-Fun Baked Apples with Granola

Prep Time: 10 Minutes • Microwave: 6 Minutes

4 servings (½ apple each)

2 **large crisp apples (such as Braeburn, Gala or Fuji)**

2 **tablespoons raisins or sweetened dried cranberries**

2 **tablespoons packed brown sugar**

4 **teaspoons butter, softened**

4 **any flavor crunchy granola bars (2 pouches from 8.9-ounce box), crushed**

Milk, cream or fruit-flavored yogurt, if you like

Utensils

- Cutting board
- Sharp knife
- Spoon
- Microwavable pie plate
- Measuring spoons
- Microwavable plastic wrap
- Fork

1 Place apples on cutting board. Using sharp knife, cut each apple in half lengthwise. Using spoon, carefully remove and discard cores. Using spoon, make at least a 1-inch channel in each apple half. Arrange apple halves cut side up in microwavable pie plate. If needed, cut thin slice from bottoms to keep apple halves from tipping.

2 Fill each apple half evenly with raisins and brown sugar; dot with butter. Cover with microwavable plastic wrap, folding back one edge ¼ inch to vent steam.

3 Microwave on High 5 to 6 minutes or until apples are tender. Check to see if tender by piercing apple with a fork. Meanwhile, crush granola bars in packages with your hands. Top each apple half with crushed granola. Serve warm with milk.

1 Serving: Calories 230; Total Fat 7g (Saturated Fat 2.5g; Trans Fat 0g); Cholesterol 10mg; Sodium 110mg; Total Carbohydrate 39g (Dietary Fiber 4g); Protein 2g **Exchanges:** ½ Starch, ½ Fruit, 1½ Other Carbohydrate, 1½ Fat **Carbohydrate Choices:** 2½

Banana Split Chocolate Mug Cake

Prep Time: 10 Minutes • Microwave: 2 Minutes
Cool: 5 Minutes • 1 mug cake

¼	cup all-purpose flour	3	tablespoons milk
2	tablespoons sugar	1	tablespoon butter, melted
2	tablespoons unsweetened baking cocoa	⅓	cup vanilla or favorite flavor ice cream
½	teaspoon baking powder	1	tablespoon hot fudge sauce
⅛	teaspoon salt	1	fresh strawberry
⅓	cup mashed banana (about 1 small)		

1 In small mixing bowl, combine flour, sugar, cocoa, baking powder and salt; stir with wooden spoon until well mixed. Using whisk, stir in banana, milk and butter until smooth. Pour into a 10-ounce microwavable mug or cup.

2 Microwave on High 1 to 2 minutes or until set and cake rises (center will have a slightly wet appearance). Cool 5 minutes. Top with ice cream, hot fudge and strawberry.

1 Mug Cake: Calories 620; Total Fat 21g (Saturated Fat 13g; Trans Fat 0.5g); Cholesterol 55mg; Sodium 770mg; Total Carbohydrate 98g (Dietary Fiber 7g); Protein 10g **Exchanges:** ½ Starch, ½ Fruit, 4½ Other Carbohydrate, 1 Milk, 2½ Fat **Carbohydrate Choices:** 6½

Utensils

- Small mixing bowl
- Dry-ingredient measuring cups
- Measuring spoons
- Wooden spoon
- Whisk
- 10-ounce microwavable mug or cup

Just for fun, add other toppings such as caramel ice cream topping, whipped cream and chopped nuts.

Smiling Sun Cupcakes

Prep Time: 30 Minutes • **Bake: 30 Minutes**
Cool: 1 Hour • **24 cupcakes**

Have an adult roll and cut the sun rays ahead of time so you can easily assemble the cupcakes. If you want brighter yellow frosting, try using gel food color instead of liquid.

1. Heat oven to 350°F (325°F for dark or nonstick pan). Line 24 regular size muffin cups with paper baking cups or spray with cooking spray. In large mixing bowl, prepare cake mix using water, oil and eggs as directed on the cake mix box (amounts will be on the box).

   Bake as directed on box for cupcakes. Use pot holders to remove pans from oven. Cool completely, about 1 hour.

2. Stir 15 drops food color into frosting until bright yellow. Frost cupcakes.

3. To form sun rays, lightly sprinkle sugar on work surface and rolling pin. Roll 4 gumdrops at a time into flat ovals about 1/8-inch thick.

   Using sharp knife, cut thin sliver off top and bottom of each oval to make rectangles. Cut each rectangle in half crosswise to make 2 squares; cut each square diagonally in half to make 2 triangles. Arrange 8 gumdrop triangles around edge of each cupcake for sun rays.

4. Using small writing tip on black icing tube, pipe sunglasses onto each cupcake. Using red gel, pipe smiling mouth onto each cupcake.

1 Cupcake (Frosted; Undecorated): Calories 240; Total Fat 11g (Saturated Fat 6g; Trans Fat 1.5g); Cholesterol 45mg; Sodium 230mg; Total Carbohydrate 33g (Dietary Fiber 0g); Protein 2g **Exchanges:** 1 Starch, 1 Other Carbohydrate, 2 Fat **Carbohydrate Choices:** 2

1 box yellow cake mix with pudding
  Water
  Vegetable oil
  Eggs
  Yellow food color
1 container vanilla creamy ready-to-spread frosting
  Sugar
48 large yellow, orange and/or red gumdrops (from 10-ounce package)
  Black decorating icing (from 4.25-ounce tube)
  Red decorating gel (from 0.68-ounce tube)

Utensils

- Large mixing bowl
- Electric mixer
- Liquid-ingredient measuring cup
- Two 12-cup muffin pans
- 24 paper baking cups
- Pot holders
- Cooling rack
- Spoon
- Rolling pin
- Ruler
- Sharp knife

133

Celebration Strawberries-and-Cream Cake Pops

Prep Time: 40 Minutes • **Bake: 30 Minutes** • **Cool: 1 Hour**
Freeze: 30 Minutes • **36 cake pops**

1 box white cake mix with pudding
Water
Vegetable oil
Egg whites
½ cup powdered sugar
2 ounces cream cheese, softened
¼ cup butter, softened

¼ cup strawberry jam
1 cup dried strawberries, chopped
1 cup red candy melts (from 14-ounce bag)
2 bags (14 ounces each) pink candy melts or coating wafers
½ cup pink sugar

Utensils

- 13×9-inch pan
- 2 large mixing bowls
- Liquid-ingredient measuring cups
- Pot holders
- Cooling rack
- Cookie sheet
- Waxed paper
- Dry-ingredient measuring cups
- Electric mixer
- Wooden spoon
- 36 paper lollipop sticks
- 1 large block white plastic foam
- Microwavable bowls

1 Heat oven to 350°F (325°F for dark or nonstick pan). Using pastry brush or paper towel, grease 13×9-inch pan. In large mixing bowl, combine cake mix, water, oil and egg whites as directed (amounts will be on the box).

Bake as directed on the box for a 13×9-inch pan. Cool completely, about 1 hour. Use pot holders to remove pan from oven.

2 Line cookie sheet with waxed paper. In large mixing bowl, beat powdered sugar, cream cheese, butter and jam with electric mixer on medium speed until blended. With your hands, crumble cake into the cream cheese mixture; mix well with wooden spoon. Stir in dried strawberries. Shape into 2-inch balls; place on cookie sheet. Freeze until firm. When cake balls are firm, transfer to refrigerator.

3 Place each color of candy melts in separate microwavable bowls. Microwave each on High 30 to 60 seconds or until melted, stirring every 20 seconds. Spoon about 2 tablespoons melted red candy into pink candy; swirl gently. Remove several cake balls from refrigerator at a time. Dip tip of 1 lollipop stick about ½ inch into melted candy, and insert stick into 1 cake ball no more than halfway. Dip each cake ball into swirled candy to cover; gently tap off excess. (Spoon more red candy into pink candy as needed.) Poke opposite end of stick into foam block. Sprinkle with pink sugar. Let stand until set.

1 Cake Pop: Calories 260; Total Fat 13g (Saturated Fat 9g; Trans Fat 0g); Cholesterol 5mg; Sodium 150mg; Total Carbohydrate 36g (Dietary Fiber 0g); Protein 1g **Exchanges:** ½ Starch, 2 Other Carbohydrate, 2½ Fat **Carbohydrate Choices:** 2½

Peach Pie Pops

Prep Time: 50 Minutes • **Bake: 13 Minutes** • **Cool: 30 Minutes** • **16 pie pops**

⅓ cup granulated sugar

2 tablespoons cornstarch

¼ teaspoon ground cinnamon

⅛ teaspoon ground nutmeg

2 large peaches

2 boxes refrigerated pie crusts, softened as directed on box

1 egg, slightly beaten

3 tablespoons white sparkling sugar

Utensils

- Cutting board
- Sharp knife
- 2-quart saucepan
- Dry-ingredient measuring cups
- Measuring spoons
- Whisk
- Wooden spoon
- 2 cookie sheets
- Cooking parchment paper
- 3½-inch round cutter
- 16 craft sticks (flat wooden sticks with round ends) or paper lollipop sticks
- Spoon
- Pastry brush
- 4-inch round cutter
- Sharp knife or pastry cutter
- Ruler
- Pot holders
- Cooling racks

1 In 2-quart saucepan, mix granulated sugar, cornstarch, cinnamon and nutmeg with whisk.

Using sharp knife, peel peaches; cut each one in half and scoop out pit with spoon. Place peaches on cutting board. Chop to measure 2 cups. Add peaches to sugar mixture; toss to coat. Cook over medium heat, stirring constantly with wooden spoon, until sauce is thick and bubbly and coats the peaches. Remove from heat. Cool completely.

2 Meanwhile, heat oven to 450°F. Line 2 cookie sheets with cooking parchment paper. Remove 2 pie crusts from pouches; unroll on floured work surface. Using a 3½-inch round cutter, cut out 8 rounds from each crust. Place 8 rounds on each cookie sheet.

3 Gently press 1 craft stick from center to edge of each round. Spoon fruit mixture evenly onto each round leaving a ½ inch edge. Brush edges with beaten egg.

4 Remove remaining 2 pie crusts from pouches; unroll on floured work surface. Using 4-inch round cutter, cut out 8 rounds from each crust. Using a sharp knife or pastry cutter, cut each round into ¼-inch-wide strips. Place half of strips ¼ inch apart over filling on each round. Weave remaining strips over and under. Seal edges with fingers. Brush strips with remaining egg. Sprinkle with sparkling sugar.

5 Bake 10 to 13 minutes or until crust is golden brown. Use pot holders to remove cookie sheets from oven. Remove from cookie sheets to cooling racks. Cool completely before serving.

1 Pie Pop: Calories 230; Total Fat 11g (Saturated Fat 4.5g; Trans Fat 0g); Cholesterol 15mg; Sodium 230mg; Total Carbohydrate 31g (Dietary Fiber 0g); Protein 2g **Exchanges:** ½ Starch, 1½ Other Carbohydrate, 2 Fat **Carbohydrate Choices:** 2

Brownies on a Stick

Prep Time: 30 Minutes • Cool: 1 Hour • Freeze: 1 Hour • 15 brownie pops

1	box supreme brownie mix with pouch of chocolate-flavor syrup
	Water
	Vegetable oil
	Egg
⅔	cup semisweet chocolate chips
1½	teaspoons shortening
	Assorted candy sprinkles

1 Heat oven to 350°F (325°F for dark or nonstick pan). Line 8-inch or 9-inch square pan with foil so foil extends about 2 inches over sides of pan. Spray foil with cooking spray.

2 In large mixing bowl, stir the brownie mix, water, vegetable oil and egg as directed on brownie mix box (amounts will be on the box).

👍 Bake as directed on box for 8- or 9-inch square pan. Remove from oven. Use pot holders to remove pan from oven. Cool completely, about 1 hour.

3 Place brownies in freezer for 30 minutes. Remove brownies from pan by lifting foil; peel foil from sides of brownies.

🔪 For bars, using sharp knife, cut into 5 rows by 3 rows. Gently insert craft stick into end of each bar, peeling foil from bars. Place on cookie sheet; freeze 30 minutes.

4 In small microwavable bowl, microwave chocolate chips and shortening uncovered on High about 1 minute; stir until smooth. If necessary, microwave an additional 5 seconds at a time. Dip the top one-third to one-half of each brownie into chocolate; sprinkle with candy sprinkles. Lay flat on waxed paper or foil to dry.

1 Brownie Pop: Calories 220; Total Fat 8g (Saturated Fat 2.5g; Trans Fat 0g); Cholesterol 15mg; Sodium 115mg; Total Carbohydrate 34g (Dietary Fiber 1g); Protein 1g **Exchanges:** ½ Starch, 2 Other Carbohydrate, 1½ Fat **Carbohydrate Choices:** 2

For a black-and-white effect, use white baking chips instead of the chocolate chips.

Utensils

- 8-inch or 9-inch square pan
- Foil
- Large mixing bowl
- Liquid-ingredient measuring cup
- Pot holders
- Cooling rack
- Sharp knife

- 15 craft sticks (flat wooden sticks with rounded ends)
- Cookie sheet
- Small microwavable bowl
- Dry-measuring cups
- Measuring spoons
- Waxed paper or foil

Bottom-of-the-Cereal-Box Cookies

Prep Time: 40 Minutes • **Bake: 10 Minutes**

2½ dozen cookies

1	pouch sugar cookie mix
½	cup butter, softened
1	egg
3	cups total of a variety of cereals (including cereal crumbs)

Utensils

- Large mixing bowl
- Wooden spoon
- Dry-ingredient measuring cups
- Measuring spoons
- Cookie sheet
- Ruler
- Pot holders
- Pancake turner
- Cooling rack

1 Heat oven to 350°F. In large mixing bowl, combine cookie mix, butter and egg; stir with wooden spoon until soft dough forms. Stir in the cereal.

2 Drop and shape dough by rounded measuring tablespoonfuls 2 inches apart onto ungreased cookie sheet.

3 Bake 8 to 10 minutes or until golden brown around edges. Use hot pads to remove cookie sheet from oven. Cool 1 minute; remove from cookie sheet to cooling rack with pancake turner.

1 Cookie: Calories 110; Total Fat 5g (Saturated Fat 2.5g; Trans Fat 0.5g); Cholesterol 15mg; Sodium 95mg; Total Carbohydrate 16g (Dietary Fiber 0g); Protein 1g **Exchanges:** 1 Starch, 1 Fat **Carbohydrate Choices:** 1

To make bars instead of cookies, make the cookie dough as directed above—except press the dough in the bottom of an ungreased 13×9-inch pan. Bake at 350°F for 20 to 25 minutes or until golden brown. Cool completely, about 1 hour, before cutting into bars.

Cook Up Cookie Fun

Treats like cookies are fun to make and fun to eat. Next time you make cookies, try adding some new ingredients either to the dough or maybe on top or in between—you get to decide!

To start, make up a pouch of your favorite cookie flavor—sugar, oatmeal or chocolate chip are all yummy choices. Use the directions on the pouch to make and bake the cookies.

Stir into the dough (before baking) one or two of these (about ½ cup of each):

Candy-coated chocolate pieces

Chopped pretzels

Chopped nuts like pecans, walnuts or mixed nuts

Chopped peanuts

Raisins or dried cranberries

Miniature marshmallows

Favorite cereal (or better yet, bottom-of-the-box crumbs!)

Colored candy sprinkles

After baking the cookies, spread the top or make sandwich cookies—try topping or filling with:

Frosting

Melted chocolate or white chocolate

Peanut butter (and jelly)

Chocolate hazelnut spread

Raspberry or strawberry preserves

Lemon curd

Marshmallow creme

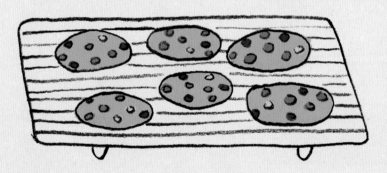

Cookie Ice Cream Sandwiches

Prep Time: 1 Hour • **Bake: 13 Minutes** • **Cool: 30 Minutes** • **12 ice cream sandwiches**

1 pouch chocolate chip cookie mix
½ cup butter, softened
1 egg
4 cups ice cream, frozen yogurt, sherbet or sorbet
Candy sprinkles or miniature chocolate chips, if you like

1 Heat oven to 375°F. In large mixing bowl, combine cookie mix, butter and egg; stir with wooden spoon until soft dough forms.

2 Drop dough by rounded tablespoonfuls 2 inches apart onto ungreased cookie sheet.

3 Bake 11 to 13 minutes or until edges are light golden brown. Use pot holders to remove cookie sheet from oven. Cool 1 minute. Remove from cookie sheet to cooling rack with pancake turner. Cool completely, about 30 minutes.

4 For each ice cream sandwich, place 1 scoop of ice cream (about ⅓ cup) between 2 cookies. Gently press cookies together (ice cream should spread to edge of cookies). Place sprinkles in shallow bowl; roll ice cream edges in sprinkles. Eat immediately, or to save for later, wrap sandwiches individually in plastic wrap. Place in resealable freezer plastic bag, and freeze until needed.

1 Ice Cream Sandwich: Calories 350; Total Fat 18g (Saturated Fat 11g; Trans Fat 0.5g); Cholesterol 60mg; Sodium 220mg; Total Carbohydrate 43g (Dietary Fiber 0g); Protein 4g **Exchanges:** 2½ Other Carbohydrate, ½ Low-Fat Milk, 3 Fat **Carbohydrate Choices:** 3

Utensils

- Large mixing bowl
- Wooden spoon
- Measuring spoons
- Cookie sheet
- Ruler
- Pot holders
- Pancake turner
- Cooling rack
- Dry-ingredient measuring cup
- Ice cream scoop
- Shallow bowl
- Plastic wrap
- Resealable freezer plastic bag

Chocolate chip sandwiches are delicious but you can use any flavor of cookie mix that you like instead of the chocolate chip mix. Vary the flavor of the ice cream, too.

145

Ghostly Cereal S'mores

Prep Time: 10 Minutes • **Stand: 1 Hour** • **24 bars**

8   cups honey graham cereal squares

Butter for greasing

5   cups miniature marshmallows ✳

1½ cups milk chocolate chips

¼   cup light corn syrup

5   tablespoons butter

1   teaspoon vanilla

1   cup miniature marshmallows, if you like

1 Measure cereal into large bowl. Butter a 13×9-inch pan and back of large spoon. In large microwavable bowl, microwave 5 cups marshmallows, the chocolate chips, corn syrup and butter uncovered on High 2 minutes to 3 minutes 30 seconds, stirring after every minute, until melted and smooth when stirred. Stir in vanilla.

2 Pour over cereal; quickly toss until completely coated. Stir in 1 cup marshmallows.

3 Press mixture evenly in pan, using buttered back of spoon. Let stand uncovered at least 1 hour, or refrigerate if you prefer a firmer bar.

For bars, using sharp knife, cut into 6 rows by 4 rows. Store loosely covered at room temperature up to 2 days.

Stove-Top Directions: Measure cereal into large bowl. Butter 13×9-inch pan and back of large spoon. In 3-quart saucepan, heat 5 cups marshmallows, the chocolate chips, corn syrup and butter over low heat, stirring occasionally, until melted; remove from heat. Stir in vanilla. Continue as directed above.

1 Bar: Calories 180; Total Fat 6g (Saturated Fat 3g; Trans Fat 0g); Cholesterol 10mg; Sodium 160mg; Total Carbohydrate 29g (Dietary Fiber 0g); Protein 2g **Exchanges:** ½ Starch, 1½ Other Carbohydrate, 1 Fat **Carbohydrate Choices:** 2

If you spray your bowl with cooking spray before using it, you'll have less mess to clean when you're done.

Utensils

- Large bowl
- Dry-ingredient measuring cup
- 13×9-inch pan
- Large spoon
- Large microwavable bowl
- Liquid-ingredient measuring cup
- Measuring spoons
- Spoon
- Sharp knife

Fruiti Sushi

Prep Time: 20 Minutes • **16 candies**

1¼ cups oven toasted rice cereal squares (gluten free)

1 cup white vanilla baking chips

4 rolls any flavor chewy fruit snack roll-ups (from 5-ounce box), unwrapped

12 candy worms

Utensils

- Dry-ingredient measuring cups
- Resealable food-storage plastic bag
- Medium microwavable bowl
- Wooden spoon
- Ruler
- Small sharp knife

1 Place cereal in resealable food-storage plastic bag; seal bag and crush with fingers to make ¾ cup.

2 In medium microwavable bowl, microwave baking chips as directed on package until melted and stirred with wooden spoon until smooth. Add crushed cereal; stir until well coated.

3 Unroll fruit snack rolls. For each sushi roll, spread one-quarter of the cereal mixture on snack roll leaving ½ inch of one short side empty. Arrange 3 candy worms, side by side, on the cereal-covered short side.

4 Starting with short side topped with candy worms, roll up each snack roll tightly, pressing unfilled short side of roll to seal. Let sushi rolls stand 5 to 10 minutes or until firm. Cut each roll into 4 slices using small sharp knife. Store loosely covered.

1 Candy: Calories 110; Total Fat 4g (Saturated Fat 3g; Trans Fat 0g); Cholesterol 0mg; Sodium 65mg; Total Carbohydrate 19g (Dietary Fiber 0g); Protein 1g **Exchanges:** ½ Starch, ½ Other Carbohydrate, 1 Fat **Carbohydrate Choices:** 1

Dance-Party Yogurt Root Beer Floats

Prep Time: 5 Minutes • Freeze: 2 Hours • 2 servings

1   container (5.3 ounces) Greek vanilla yogurt

2   cans root beer, chilled

Utensils

- Measuring spoons
- Ice cube tray
- 2 tall serving glasses

1 Place about 1 tablespoon yogurt into each of 8 sections of ice cube tray. Freeze about 2 hours or until firm.

2 In 2 tall serving glasses, place 4 yogurt ice cubes each. Pour root beer over cubes. Serve immediately.

1 Serving: Calories 50; Total Fat 0g (Saturated Fat 0g; Trans Fat 0g); Cholesterol 0mg; Sodium 90mg; Total Carbohydrate 6g (Dietary Fiber 0g); Protein 7g **Exchanges:** ½ Skim Milk, ½ Very Lean Meat **Carbohydrate Choices:** ½

Use an ice cube tray that makes fun shapes like stars and hearts.

erry

Green Grape

Papaya

Cherry

Blueberry

Orange

Utensils

- Blender
- Dry-ingredient measuring cups
- Measuring spoons
- Six 5-ounce paper cups
- Foil
- Craft sticks

These pops can also be made with strawberries, grapefruit, plums, mango or pineapple.

Fruity Frozen Yogurt Pops

Prep Time: 10 Minutes • Freeze: 6 Hours • 6 pops

2 containers (6 ounces each) low-fat French vanilla yogurt

2 cups cut-up fresh fruit such as blueberries, bananas, cherries, grapes, papaya, peaches, oranges or raspberries

1 tablespoon honey

1 In blender, place all ingredients. Cover blender and blend until smooth.

2 Divide mixture among 6 paper cups. Cover cups with foil; insert craft stick into center of each pop. (Or, if you like, fill ice pop molds according to manufacturer's directions.) Freeze about 6 hours or until frozen. To serve, peel away paper cups.

1 Pop: Calories 110; Total Fat 1g (Saturated Fat 0g; Trans Fat 0g); Cholesterol 0mg; Sodium 35mg; Total Carbohydrate 22g (Dietary Fiber 1g); Protein 3g **Exchanges:** 1 Starch, ½ Fruit **Carbohydrate Choices:** 1½

Shake-It-Up Chocolate Ice Cream

Prep Time: 15 Minutes
2 servings (¾ cup each)

6	cups ice cubes
½	cup kosher (coarse) salt
1	cup half-and-half
2	tablespoons sugar
1	tablespoon hot fudge sauce
½	teaspoon vanilla

Utensils

- Dry-ingredient measuring cups
- 1-gallon resealable plastic bag
- Liquid-ingredient measuring cup
- Measuring spoons
- 1-quart food-storage freezer bag

1. Place ice and salt in 1-gallon resealable freezer plastic bag; shake to mix.

2. Place half and half, sugar, hot fudge and vanilla in 1-quart food-storage plastic bag; seal tightly. Knead bag until well mixed.

3. Place bag with half-and-half mixture inside gallon bag with ice; seal tightly. Put on gloves or oven mitts because bags will be very cold. Shake bags about 5 minutes or until mixture hardens. Serve immediately. You can discard the ice and salt when you are done making ice cream.

1 Serving: Calories 250; Total Fat 15g (Saturated Fat 9g; Trans Fat 0g); Cholesterol 45mg; Sodium 85mg; Total Carbohydrate 24g (Dietary Fiber 0g); Protein 4g **Exchanges:** 1½ Starch, 3 Fat **Carbohydrate Choices:** 1½

For cookies 'n cream flavored ice cream, omit the hot fudge and add ½ cup coarsely crushed chocolate sandwich cookies (about 6 cookies).

It's the combination of the ice and salt that makes the mixture freeze.

Metric Conversion Guide

Volume

U.S. UNITS	CANADIAN METRIC	AUSTRALIAN METRIC
¼ teaspoon	1 mL	1 ml
½ teaspoon	2 mL	2 ml
1 teaspoon	5 mL	5 ml
1 tablespoon	15 mL	20 ml
¼ cup	50 mL	60 ml
⅓ cup	75 mL	80 ml
½ cup	125 mL	125 ml
⅔ cup	150 mL	170 ml
¾ cup	175 mL	190 ml
1 cup	250 mL	250 ml
1 quart	1 liter	1 liter
1½ quarts	1.5 liters	1.5 liters
2 quarts	2 liters	2 liters
2½ quarts	2.5 liters	2.5 liters
3 quarts	3 liters	3 liters
4 quarts	4 liters	4 liters

Weight

U.S. UNITS	CANADIAN METRIC	AUSTRALIAN METRIC
1 ounce	30 grams	30 grams
2 ounces	55 grams	60 grams
3 ounces	85 grams	90 grams
4 ounces (¼ pound)	115 grams	125 grams
8 ounces (½ pound)	225 grams	225 grams
16 ounces (1 pound)	455 grams	500 grams
1 pound	455 grams	0.5 kilogram

Note: The recipes in this cookbook have not been developed or tested using metric measures. When converting recipes to metric, some variations in quality may be noted.

Measurements

INCHES	CENTIMETERS
1	2.5
2	5.0
3	7.5
4	10.0
5	12.5
6	15.0
7	17.5
8	20.5
9	23.0
10	25.5
11	28.0
12	30.5
13	33.0

Temperatures

FAHRENHEIT	CELSIUS
32°	0°
212°	100°
250°	120°
275°	140°
300°	150°
325°	160°
350°	180°
375°	190°
400°	200°
425°	220°
450°	230°
475°	240°
500°	260°

Index

Recipe Testing and Calculating Nutrition Information

Recipe Testing:

- Large eggs and 2% milk were used unless otherwise indicated.

- Fat-free, low-fat, low-sodium or lite products were not used unless indicated.

- No nonstick cookware and bakeware were used unless otherwise indicated. No dark-colored, black or insulated bakeware was used.

- When a pan is specified, a metal pan was used; a baking dish or pie plate means ovenproof glass was used.

- An electric hand mixer was used for mixing only when mixer speeds are specified.

Calculating Nutrition:

- The first ingredient was used wherever a choice is given, such as $\frac{1}{3}$ cup sour cream or plain yogurt.

- The first amount was used wherever a range is given, such as 3- to 3½-pound whole chicken.

- The first serving number was used wherever a range is given, such as 4 to 6 servings.

- "If desired" ingredients were not included.

- Only the amount of a marinade or frying oil that is absorbed was included.